gekocht
5.30 g.
vertrek
gelezen

C000040665

COUNTRIES IN THIS SERIES

THE SIMPLE GUIDE TO

VIETNAM

CUSTOMS & ETIQUETTE

COVER ILLUSTRATION

Taking fruit to market on the Mekong Delta

ABOUT THE AUTHOR

GEOFFREY MURRAY has spent a quarter of a century in the Far East as a business journalist/analyst, including 16 years in Japan, five in Singapore and four in China. He has been decorated by the Australian Government for his work as a war correspondent in Vietnam, and has recently returned there to complete this book. His other publications include *Vietnam: Dawn of a New Market* (1997) and *Singapore: The Global City State* (1996).

Ancestral altar statuettes, Hanoi

ILLUSTRATED BY
IRENE SANDERSON

THE SIMPLE GUIDE TO

VIETNAM

CUSTOMS & ETIQUETTE

Geoffrey Murray

GLOBAL BOOKS LTD

Simple Guides • Series 1
CUSTOMS & ETIQUETTE

The Simple Guide to
VIETNAM
CUSTOMS & ETIQUETTE

First published 1997 by
Global Books Ltd
PO Box 219, Folkestone, Kent CT20 3LZ, England

ISBN 1–86034–090–3

British Library Cataloguing in Publication Data
A CIP catalogue entry for this book
is available from the British Library.

Distributed in the USA & Canada by:
The Talman Co., Inc., New York

Set in Futura 11 on 12 pt by Bookman, Slough
Printed in Great Britain by
The Cromwell Press, Broughton Gifford, Wiltshire

Contents

1

People & History

Halong Bay, northern Vietnam

What is Vietnam and who are the Vietnamese? The answers are complex. It is a country with an expanding but fragile economy, being developed by a battle-hardened people able to endure great hardships. It is a country whose government for years has epitomized to the West an ideological hardness, yet has also demonstrated the most remarkable pragmatism. It is a country built on fierce national pride, but at the same time is capable of demonstrating openness to new, foreign ideas, which it is doing to an increasing extent.

The Vietnamese have inherited many foreign influences over the centuries. In the north, a people forced to accept Chinese hegemony, either by paying tribute to the Emperor or having to accept periodic occupation, would then become strong enough to throw off the yoke of foreign oppression repeatedly only to have to face fresh foreign incursions once again.

A key exhibit in the Historical Museum in Hanoi is a record of these triumphs. Streets in the capital and Ho Chi Minh City (Saigon) are named after important historical figures who resisted the Chinese. Among these heroes are Hai Ba Trung (the Trung Sisters who led a three-year rebellion in AD40-43 before being killed) and Le Loi, who ended Vietnam's subjection as a vassal state of the Ming Dynasty and helped create the Later Le Dynasty (1427-1789) when traditional Vietnamese culture was able to flourish unfettered.

From China came the influences of Confucianism and Taoism and from India Hinduism. Buddhism, too, entered from both directions. Catholicism arrived in the early 1500s, in the shape of Jesuit priests from the Portuguese colony of Macao. Later, the French and Dutch caused the rulers of the Le Dynasty much concern, as they (rightly as it happened) saw Western missionaries as importers of subversive ideas.

Modern Vietnam began to emerge when land-hungry Viets spilled out of the crowded Red River valley around Hanoi before the fifteenth century, going on to defeat the Cham people on the central coast and colonizing the south in the seventeenth and eighteenth centuries. The Chams were a Hindu-worshipping people who had close links with Indian culture through trade and through the Khmer people of what is now Cambodia, and were virtually untouched by Chinese influences. With the advance of the Viets, however, Cham culture was quickly submerged.

A Vietnamese sense of identity was further honed by resistance to French rule from the late nineteenth century to 1954 – with a brief interlude of brutal Japanese occupation during the Second World War; finally, there was the struggle against the United States, which ended in the reunification of the country in 1975.

Family transport

Visiting Vietnam today, especially once the traveller has left the environs of the two major cities, where most of the economic development has been concentrated, it is easy to find evidence of backwardness and poverty. But it has to be remembered that the people of Vietnam have been at war, either overtly or covertly, more or less continuously from 1850 until 1979 (the invasion of Cambodia).

The French colonialists thoroughly exploited Vietnam's natural resources. Vast rubber, coffee and sugar plantations were established exclusively to serve export markets. Indigenous industries were supplanted in favour of imports from France. Crushing taxes and land requisition for the administration's favourites created a vast army of landless peasants for eventual conscription into French-run mines and factories both in Vietnam and in France itself. The exploitation continued during the Japanese occupation when Vietnam was forced to contribute food, cash and other resources to the Japanese war effort.

For a variety of geopolitical reasons, North Vietnam found its chief allies in the Communist world in its struggle to cling to independence after the Second World War. After final victory in 1975, a reuinified Vietnam followed the socialist model of the former Soviet Union, and this continues to exert a strong influence. Thus, Marx has been added to Confucius as a conditioning factor on national behaviour.

Given the historical background, visitors to Vietnam today will find a proud and independent people who do little to puncture the notion that they are special. They like to play up the 'David and Goliath' mystique to outsiders and perhaps half-believe it themselves. How else would they have dared to take on France, America and China?

Some writers have suggested that Vietnam illustrates the 'younger brother' syndrome. With a much bigger neighbour, China, it has been forced to display all the tenacity and seeking after attention, whether positive or negative, that typifies the behaviour of younger male siblings the world over. It may seem a bit fanciful but it is an idea that has some merit in explaining Vietnamese behaviour.

The bulk of the population occupy two bulges at each end of the country. In the south, communities developed along the maze of channels and canals that form the Mekong Delta, where the mighty Mekong River starting in China's Yunnan Province finally emerges from Cambodia and heads for the south. It brings down with it a great deal of rich alluvial soil that makes the growing of rice, and a vast array of fruits and vegetables, a relatively easy task. Thus, southerners have never had to strive hard to make a living, which has earned them a reputation for being lazy.

In the north, a similar pattern of colonization grew up around the delta of the Red River, which also starts in Yunnan Province and passes through Hanoi and reaches the sea at the present port of Haiphong, again depositing vast alluvial deposits in the final stages of its journey for agriculture to flourish.

But the north is also rich in anthracite coal and a vast treasure-house of minerals such as iron ore, copper, lead, bauxite, chromium, tin, tungsten and gold, along with fine clay for porcelain. Yet the people in the north have had to struggle much harder for their survival and have known periods of famine which the south has been spared. This has created a certain additional toughness in north-erners, who tend to regard southerners as 'soft'.

On the whole, the people of Hanoi are thought to be more talkative and philosophical, but are also more elusive when answering questions. Northern Vietnamese are also somewhat more traditional and still hold the family and the longevity of old age in high esteem. Hanoians are also said to be a little more laid back and calmer than their somewhat frenetic southern counterparts for whom making money in any way possible seems to be a major preoccupation.

Temple courtyard, Ho Chi Minh City

It is said that if a Saigonese won a lottery jackpot of, say, $1000, he or she would most probably buy presents for their families, purchasing clothing, foodstuffs and other luxury items. Someone in Hanoi, however, would be more likely to feel that the money should be spent on necessities like 'fixing the roof' and 'buying new kitchen utensils'.

2

Legends & Beliefs

Young campaigner, Saigon

According to legend, Vietnam was founded as a result of a dragon's loneliness. It seems that the wandering dragon, an ancient symbol of good fortune, came upon a land of unsurpassed beauty. He then assumed human form, married the daughter of the local dragon lord and produced a son named Lac Long Quan. The latter, who is credited with creating an agriculturally-based, organized society, eventually married an immortal princess named Au Co and their union produced 100 sons born simultaneously from 100 eggs.

Because of the inevitable overcrowding, the family split up. Half the sons stayed with Au Co near present-day Hanoi, one of them founding the first Vietnamese dynasty, the Hung, some time in the first millennium BC. The remainder stayed with their father in the south, although eventually Lac and Au Co were to be reunited in the spirit world. Reflecting these romantic origins, the earliest name for Vietnam was Au Lac.

Whether or not a Chinese dragon did travel south, the fact is that real Chinese (from the start of the Han Dynasty in the second century BC) soon began to find their way through the protective mountain chain to begin a millennium of domination. Interbreeding followed which created the racial mix that became the dominant Viets. It is this cultural strain that survives, having almost totally submerged that of the Cham, whose Champa kingdom flourished in the south (centred on an area encompassed by the present-day cities of Hue and Da Nang) from the second century AD until the mid-seventeenth century. Apart from the Indian and Khmer influences, the Chams, until at least the tenth century, also had close contacts with Java, with whose people they shared important ethnic links.

The Hinduism of the Chams later became blended with Islamic beliefs, brought in by the Arab traders for whom Vietnam was a regular stop on their travels to China, along with some aspects of animism. Some of the remaining Chams and ethnic Khmers are Muslim today, although in a somewhat diluted form.

Top Tip: A Religious People

Although there is a tendency to assume that because Vietnam is ruled by a Communist party, its people must be atheist, there are in fact quite strong religious impulses that still govern much of daily life, along with an inheritance of ancient practices. About two-thirds of the population would regard themselves as Buddhist in some form or other, but into the cultural melting pot one must also add Confucian and Taoist principles, ancestor worship and animism.

Catholic refugees fled south when the country was last partitioned, fearing oppression under the new Communist rulers because of Christianity's connections with Western powers. It was a fear actively encouraged by the US-supported South Vietnamese government seeking a staunch anti-Communist bloc. Catholics now constitute an estimated 10 per cent of the population, primarily located in and around Ho Chi Minh City (Saigon). Despite their fears, the Catholics have been able to continue to practise their faith, although there are some restrictions on the import of religious material and proselytizing is discouraged.

Buddhism is represented in two main forms reflecting the country's historic development. In the north, the predominant sect is Mahayana which developed in China and Japan before being brought south. The Khmers, many of whom settled in the Mekong Delta when the area was part of the dominant Khmer (Cambodian) kingdom, brought with them the Theravada form of Buddhism which represents the Indian influence. Also found in the south is a small mendicant form of the religion.

There are two unique native religions which are worth mentioning. Opinion is divided over whether the *Hoa Hao*, set up in 1939, is a form of Buddhism or not. Its founder, known as the 'mad monk' by the French, created a simple form of worship which dispensed with the need of an intermediary – i.e., the Abbot (*bonze*) or the monks that one normally sees officiating in pagodas around the country – and it quickly won adherents in the southern part of the country. Unfortunately, in the 1960s, due to having dabbled too much in South Vietnam's political and military affairs, the founder was executed and the sect banned for some years.

Slightly older, and even more peculiar, is *Cao Daism* (Holy See), created by a Vietnamese civil servant in the French bureaucracy to bring together a delightful pastiche of Buddhism, Confucianism, Taoism, Christianity, Islam and ancestor worship under one supreme being, the Cao Dai. The group's symbol is a single eye surrounded by the sun's rays. It has a pope supported by female cardinals. The faith also boasts a bewildering pantheon of saints including Jesus Christ, the French writer Victor Hugo, Joan of Arc and Napoleon Bonaparte.

The headquarters of Holy See is at Tay Ninh, an 80-kilometre drive Northwest of Ho Chi Minh towards the Cambodian border. The Cao Dai, with an estimated two million followers, had its own army of 25,000 men up to the mid-1960s, when it was suppressed by the generals who assumed power in a bewildering succession of coup d'etats in Saigon.

Readers of Graham Greene's *The Quiet American* may recall the Cao Dai playing an important side role in the story, the author describing the scene in Tay Ninh as 'Saint Victor Hugo, Christ and Buddha looking down from the roof of the Cathedral on a Walt Disney fantasia of the East, dragons and snakes in technicolour'.

Hue mausoleum dragon

Whatever their basic religious beliefs, a large proportion of the population continue to engage in ancestor worship, reflecting the great importance Vietnamese attach to strong family bonds and the existence of the extended family. As elsewhere in the region, Vietnamese believe that the soul lives on to maintain a protective watch over those who follow in the family line. To neglect due care and attention of the soul is to condemn it to an aimless wandering around the Kingdom of the Dead, while inviting disaster upon its descendants. Due to the disruptions of the prolonged Vietnam War, in which millions lost their lives, it is feared that there are a great many lonely souls wandering around unclaimed.

Mainly through the family altar in the home, the death anniversary is commemorated by special ceremonies, as well as during the various lunar calendar festivals referred to elsewhere. Traditionally, families have sought to have a piece of land which can become the ancestral burial ground, and the care of the graves is an important duty for the descendants.

As in China, the birth of a son is important because ancient custom has determined that only a male descendant can fulfil all the requirements of ancestor worship. The growth of urbanization and the mass movement of young people away from the countryside to the cities in search of work and a better life is placing some strain on these ancestral links, but they survive for now.

Top Tip: Taoist Belief System

Despite the seeming modernization of Vietnam, especially in the cities, the majority of people still believe to some extent in spirits who must be placated. Within these old animistic beliefs are blended some of the elements of Taoism (*Tao: The Way*), the religious system extolling virtue and humility founded by the great Chinese sage Lao Tze in the sixth century BC and brought in by the early Chinese invaders. Through study of the Tao, one is able to gain insight into the mysteries of heaven and their influence on earthly activities.

Many superstitions and ceremonies have sprung up, although these can vary from one region to another. Astrology, geomancy (divination from the shapes formed by a handful of earth thrown on the ground) and numerology (study of numbers to forecast the future) all continue to play a role in individual actions.

Top Tip: Lucky Numbers

A person's lucky numbers depend on the time, day and year when he or she was born and are determined by a numerologist. As in the West, 13 is generally considered an unlucky number, as is the number three – hence it might not be considered propitious to make important new commitments or undertake a major task on the 3rd, 13th or 23rd of the lunar month; and never try and take a photograph of three Vietnamese together!

Nine, however, is considered lucky. Fortunately, it is possible to consult a lunar calendar to check for the right moment to take key actions.

3

Anniversaries & Festivals

Altar inside Cao Dai Cathedral, Tay Ninh province

There are eight official national holidays in Vietnam, of which the most important is *Tet*, the lunar New Year festival which usually falls between late January and mid-February. This officially involves a three-day break, but the anticipation and preparations are likely to begin at least a month in advance and celebrations can drag on for a week in some form or another.

*T*et is a time for visiting, with a great deal of emphasis on the sort of 'first-footing' practised at New Year in places like Scotland. All the family, business and social acquaintances tend to visit each other at some stage during the holiday. Astrologers are often consulted because the first person to enter the house on the first day of Tet sets the conditions for the household for the coming year.

*T*here is no reason why a foreigner should not be invited to make this important first visit, but it is important that he or she is aware of the significance of the action. It may well be better to politely decline if there is any suspicion that the invitation has been extended purely out of courtesy, especially as one probably would not want to take the blame for any bad luck which the family might suffer in the coming year.

Top Tip: Avoid 'Bad Luck' Talk

One should be careful to avoid speaking ill of anyone on the first day of the New Year celebration as this will encourage a year of bad luck. In traditional belief, the first sound heard on this day can also set the tone, a dog barking, for example, portends while a rooster crowing does not, although it is no longer clear why this should be so.

---

*T*et is a time for gift-giving, the presentation of envelopes (usually pink) with new bank notes (known as *li xi* in the south and *mung tuoi* in the north); this practice is also found in China and other countries of the region with large Chinese communities such as Singapore. The envelopes are usually presented to all children, and can also be extended to cover domestic staff, subordinates and anyone younger than the giver as discretion dictates. They should never be given to anyone older! The amount of money in the envelope does not have to be large, it being more of symbolic value in wishing good fortune to the recipient.

Gifts other than money can also be given, especially to business contacts, staff and family friends. The choice would probably lie with something that the giver knew was in short supply in the country but readily available back home. Money and presents from *Viet Kieu* (overseas Vietnamese) will also be pouring in to relatives left behind by the former mass emigrations, so that this is a time of year when Vietnam looks at its most prosperous.

This, incidentally, is not a good time to do any shopping, as heavy demand tends to push up prices. And anyone visiting Vietnam on business should avoid doing so before or just after the festival as it is very unlikely that appointments can be made or honoured.

In the work environment, staff should be given a year-end bonus and also allowed time off not just for the official three days, but perhaps longer, given the fact that many may wish to visit families in other parts of the country which is likely to be a time-consuming process due to the poor state of public transportation.

For many, *Tet* is symbolized by peach and apricot trees that each household purchases for decoration and which are thought to help in warding off evil spirits. Northerners tend to attach most symbolism to the pink peach blossom, while the yellow apricot is considered more suitable for southerners. Thus, if one is going to give such a present to an acquaintance, it could be advisable to find out his or her geographical origins.

In preparation for the celebrations, houses, especially the kitchens, are rigorously cleaned and repaired, debts paid off, sins forgiven, enemies conciliated, and everything done to appease the spirits and start the new year off on a good footing.

Traditional foods are cooked in advance, as these foods take time to prepare and it is not considered proper to cook during the festival. The most popular item consumed in large quantities at this time is *banh trung*, a sticky rice cake wrapped in a banana leaf and steamed for 24 hours. *Tet*, in fact, is a time when food and drink seems to be consumed almost continually from morning until night, so that a little pre and post-festival fasting may not go amiss!

Although Christmas is not officially acknowledged in Vietnam, traditional celebrations do occur in the country. Catholic cathedrals in Hanoi and Ho Chi Minh City are filled to capacity and beyond for midnight mass on Christmas Eve. The international New Year is a public holiday in Vietnam, but there are no special celebrations.

On 30 April each year, the anniversary of the liberation of Saigon in 1975 is marked by a public holiday. Most celebrations surrounding this anniversary are limited to government activities, although the holiday is welcome in that it provides a neat break from work, being followed immediately by International Labour Day (1 May), which is also a public holiday. Vietnamese often cele-

Mid-autumn festival of Hoi An

brate by spending the day at parks with their children, on a picnic or just feasting at home. Most offices close for these holidays, although many shops, restaurants and bars remain open.

The birthday of Ho Chi Minh, founder and first president of North Vietnam, which falls on 19 May is marked by official celebrations, but it is not a public holiday.

Another double holiday occurs in September. First is National Day, on 2 September when Ho Chi Minh declared the creation of an independent state of Vietnam in Hanoi in 1945. This is a good time to send gifts to business acquaintances, joint venture partners, government offices and ministries. This is followed on 3 September by the anniversary of Ho's death in 1969. Actually, he died on the previous day, but the announcement was delayed so as not to mar the National Day festivities.

Of a more cultural/religious nature, Wandering Souls Day (*Trung Nguyen*) occurs in August and is regarded as the second most important festival after *Tet*. On this occasion, as in other Asian societies, families may visit temples or pagodas to pray for the souls of the departed, both one's own ancestors as well as the dead who may have no living descendants to perform the duty. As in China, joss papers are burnt and special foods are cooked and offered to the wandering souls.

The spring counterpart to this commemoration, incidentally, is *Thanh Minh*, on the fifth day of the third lunar month (calculated from the date on which the moveable feast of *Tet* occurs), which is marked by visits to tidy the graves of one's ancestors and pray to them.

The mid-autumn, or mini-Tet (*Trung Thu*), a month after Wandering Souls Day, is primarily for children. Mooncakes are eaten, and the occasion celebrated with noisy and colourful street processions.

On the 10th Day of the 10th lunar month, people in many areas celebrate the end of the harvest. Whereas on *Trung Thu* the presents are given to the children, this time the flow is reversed. Apart from children giving their parents gifts, it is also considered appropriate in many communities for patients to express their thanks to their doctors and pupils to their teachers in a similar way.

In addition, there are also special days and festivals peculiar to ethnic minorities and specific regions that are reminders of the country's rich and varied cultural origins.

4

Town & Country

Ho Chi Minh City

Anyone travelling around the teeming streets of Ho Chi Minh City will quickly appreciate its biggest problem: too many people! Natural growth is swelled by an influx of peasants lured away from back-breaking work in the rice paddies in the hope of richer pickings.

The city authorities are now intent on easing the strain by building six satellite new towns to the east and south, each with its own industrial estate to keep residents from flocking back to the main city in search of jobs. By 2010, when the towns are due to be completed, the population of the southern conurbation is forecast to be over seven million. But in the actual city area, the number will have been reduced from well over four million to three million or so, which the existing and planned basic infrastructure should be capable of handling.

District One, the inner city area on the northern bank of the Saigon River, retains some of its old charm with wide boulevards and a mixture of graceful colonial-style buildings from the French era now beginning to be overshadowed by a new generation of towering hotels and office blocks.

From there, tree-lined streets stretch out to the suburbs, where the charm soon disappears. Streets are choked with a mass of traffic assailing the ears with revving engines and tooting horns from early morning until the small hours of night. Housing development follows no pattern, with homes in pleasing architectural styles jammed up against grubby, ramshackle workshops in an endless low-rise strip development.

Hanoi is slightly less frenetic. Conservationists are trying to preserve the best of the ancient old quarter of the 1,000-year-old city and the gems of the French colonial period. The small opera house built by the French in 1911 and still equipped with the original mouldings and red-plush seats, is being restored. Old French villas on quiet, tree-shaded streets are coveted for renovation as up-market offices and residences.

Built around a series of picturesque lakes, Hanoi then sprawls out over the Red River, where a dike now protects the city from the former threat of devastating floods, into the surrounding rich, flat countryside. Once outside the old city, concrete tends to rule, for the market economy has completely changed the landscape and officials are having trouble regulating the growth.

Whole districts of old buildings with a dis-tinctive Vietnamese architectural character are being swept away to make room for modern developments, especially in meeting the demand for office blocks and hotels of an ever-increasing foreign business community, and new housing for a growing population now over three million.

The scars of American bombing during the Vietnam war have all but disappeared from the capital. The most famous reminder of that era that remained for many years – the so-called 'Hanoi Hilton', the jail where American pilots were kept as prisoners-of-war – has gone, to be replaced by a new hotel.

Vietnam offers a contrast between a 3,260 km coastline with a succession of stunning, almost untouched beaches (although suffering from city detritus dumped in the waters and washed up along the coastline) and natural wonders such as Ha Long Bay, where some 3,000 limestone islands in a vast array of grotesque shapes climb vertically out of the sea, to wild mountains along the Laotian border where tigers once freely roamed.

In the south, the best known resort is Vung Tau, which in French times was known as Cap St Jacques and was a popular weekend retreat for foreign residents of Saigon wishing to escape the steamy heat of the capital for more balmy parts. It was a pleasant drive of no more than 100 kilometres to loll on the golden sands and contemplate a delightful dinner of freshly-caught lobster or other sea food to be found just off the coast.

Later, it was a popular in-country r & r (rest and recreation) centre for American and Australian troops during the war, and its port a key logistics channel for the vast amounts of equipment and food needed to keep the armies in the field. Today, those lolling under beach umbrellas tend to be local, while the city is the headquarters of a vast offshore oil-drilling programme.

Further north is Cam Ranh Bay, a giant US naval and air base during the war, subsequently used by the Russian navy, which boasts an outstanding beach, as does Nha Trang, whose numerous offshore islands offer good opportunities for fisher-men and divers.

Da Nang also looms large in any history of the Vietnam War as a key military logistics site and the place (China Beach, several miles long) where American marines stormed ashore in 1965 to mark an escalating and ultimately disastrous US military involvement in the Vietnamese conflict. Just inland are the five stone hills and caves of Marble Mountain, sacred alike to the Chams, Buddhists and Viet Cong guerrillas.

Further north is Hue, the former imperial capital (1802-1945) on the banks of the Perfume River, and a noted cultural, religious and educational centre. Hue suffered grievously from French military depredations in 1885 and again during the Tet Offensive in 1968, when the Americans had a bitter struggle to retake the city from Communist occupation. Happily, the much-damaged old Imperial City is now being restored.

Hai Van Pass

It is only 80 kilometres by road between Da Nang and Hue, but the route is a difficult one, climbing as it does over the notorious Hai Van Pass (1,172 metres). For centuries it was this mountain barrier which kept the Viets and Chams apart. Appalling weather conditions, with snap flooding and landslides, add to the driving hazards of an extremely difficult road covering some 20 kilometres on each side of the 'Pass In The Clouds'. Many truck drivers find it obligatory to present flower and incense offerings on the altars at the top of the pass and pray to the mountain god for a safe passage. Soon, this will be a memory when a series of three road tunnels creates a straight route under the pass.

The central coastal region from the beautiful beaches of Phan Thiet up to the Ben Hai River, marking the dividing line between North and South Vietnam until 1975, also contains many relics of the Champa empire.

Top Tip: Tigers and Highlands

In sharp contrast to the hot and humid coast, are the cool, fresh mountains of the Central Highlands, where rich volcanic soil has nurtured some of the country's best coffee plantations. There are four principal towns worth visiting – Da Lat, adjacent to an imperial hunting reserve of thick pine forests full of tigers, elephants and deer and a summer retreat for French colonial officials from Saigon, Buon Me Thuot, Pleiku and Kontum. The area is still populated by various hill tribes who manage to maintain many aspects of their traditional way of life, colourful dress and unique customs.

Various ethnic groups also occupy the mountains separating Vietnam from China in the far north. The areas are among the poorest in the country, but boast magnificent scenery and are worth visiting if one is prepared to tolerate an extremely difficult journey over poor roads lasting many hours.

At the other end of the country, the Mekong Delta's rich vegetation and maze of river channels and canals offers a rich and fascinating history, being the hiding place for political exiles and religious apostates, pirates and smugglers, and, latterly, Viet Cong guerrillas. The main towns are Can Tho and My Tho, within relatively easy reach of Ho Chi Minh City.

Less accessible, but worth visiting if for no other reason than for the wide variety of shrimps it breeds, is Ca Mau on the southern tip of the country. It lies in a vast mangrove swamp known as the U-Minh Forest, although wartime defoliation has destroyed some of the beauty of this wilderness area. From here, those with time can also explore some of the unspoilt nearby islands including Phu Quoc, noted for its fine beaches and the quality of its *nuoc mam* fish sauce. More sinister is the former penal colony island of Con Son, where prisoners were kept in cages in appalling conditions.

5

Travel Tips

The bus into town

For the moment, most of the still limited number of foreign tourists arrive in Vietnam looking to revive or exorcise wartime memories, or searching for history, rather than seeking sun-kissed beaches or unspoilt and mysterious mist-enshrouded mountain peaks – although these certainly exist.

Whatever the motive of the would-be visitor, however, the first thing which must be stressed is that one should not go to Vietnam with extremely high expectations as regards comfort and convenience.

The tourism industry in Vietnam is still in the fledgling stage. As money becomes available, the country is trying to overhaul its badly neglected, and heavily war-damaged, road and rail network. There is also a need for more qualified and better trained service staff and management. But this is only to be expected in a country where there was no service industry to speak of for almost a generation. In addition, although economic development is accelerating fairly rapidly, Vietnam remains a relatively poor country by most people's standards.

This may be one reason why foreign visitors tend to face a dual pricing system, having to pay two, three or even many times more for virtually everything compared to the local population, even though the level of service offered may be no different. This includes hotel rooms, meals, domestic travel, especially by air, tours, and entrance tickets to places of interest like museums and temples. This practice is based on the assumption that the visitor is rich and can readily afford to pay the inflated price.

Top Tip: Patience etc is a Virtue

The most important attributes needed when visiting Vietnam are a strong sense of humour, patience and calm.

Top Tip: The Cost of Appearance

Visitors learn very quickly that it can pay to dress down in Vietnam. Despite officially-set rates and tariffs, the actual charge for some services can depend on one's appearance. If you look wealthy, or 'executive', or show that you are an inexperienced international traveller, then the price tends to be high. A tourist looking less prosperous, perhaps carrying a battered rucksack, and, even better, able to speak a few words of Vietnamese, can often end up paying less.

Vietnamese are a friendly people who don't appreciate foreigners who want to keep their distance. Actually, by mixing with the locals and behaving in a simple, straightforward manner, one can often see and understand more about the country than those on group or package tours, who may well enjoy a more relaxing time but eventually leave the country feeling slightly disappointed that they have missed out on something important.

Following a recent construction boom, newly-built international standard hotels in Hanoi, Ho Chi Minh City and some other major towns are now facing a glut of rooms and severe shortage of visitors, with occupancy rates as low as 30 per cent.

Vietnam's first post-war international standard project in the south was the Saigon Floating Hotel, towed in complete on a barge from Australia's Great Barrier Reef; the initial, very successful five-year lease was renewed at the end of 1994. Since then, major hotel chains from various countries have moved into the four and five-star end of the market around District 1, the city centre, remarkably unchanged from the height of the Vietnam War, creating a total capacity of around 5,500 rooms.

Hanoi has a lot of catching up to do, but plans are in place to build 33 'international standard' hotels of between three and five stars, mostly around the capital's various very attractive lakes, providing a total of about 5,000 rooms by 1998.

Mekong riverscape

Both cities want more. Ho Chi Minh thinks it will need 21,000 rooms by the turn of the century, while Hanoi more modestly aims for 10,000. But none of the rooms now on offer comes cheap, and many visitors on tight budgets find it better to go to the main streets in search of the rash of 'mini-hotels'. With land costs high, these hotels tend to be tall and thin, typically one room wide and two deep. But the limited number of rooms available still offer most of the basic comforts, such as en suite bathrooms, telephone and television, and even a refrigerator.

What may not be on offer is food cooked on the premises. But it is easy to find a decent restaurant down the street, and many of the hotels often have an arrangement with a nearby establishment to have meals brought in for the guest, especially breakfast. Below the mini-hotels are even cheaper guest houses and rooms for rent which enjoy good business.

In travelling around Vietnam it is worth remembering that this is a country which in 1995 had an installed electricity capacity of only 3,500 megawatts, no more than 500,000 telephone lines and a crumbling road network of which only 40 per cent is paved. Much of the basic infrastructure development has been in the two main cities.

The railways are in a sorry state. Most of the rolling stock is either steam-driven Chinese locomotives or Russian diesel-driven engines dating from the 1960s which were sold to Vietnam some years ago by the Belgians. The train system that links Hanoi to Ho Chi Minh City, and provides affordable transport to a large number of people, has slowly got better. What was a 72-hour journey in 1989 now *only* takes 36 hours!

The continued relative slowness is caused by the poor condition of the track, lack of modern signalling equipment and the delicate state of locomotives and carriages that would not be able to survive anything above pedestrian speed. The same applies to the lines beteen Hanoi and the major port of Haiphong, at the mouth of the Red River, and to Lao Cai, on the border with China. But rail travel is only an option for those with a great deal of time and a strong commitment to 'experiencing life in the raw'.

Vietnam has about 10,000 kilometres of roads, most of which suffered from war damage and neglect. Forty per cent of them are rated 'poor' or 'very poor'. There are 8,280 bridges half of which are dilapidated. Upgrading and repair has begun but it will be years before a decent road network is in place.

Top Tip: Beware of 'Road Rage'

For anyone wishing to make a long road journey the emphasis has to be on the word 'long'. High speeds are impossible on most roads, although that does not stop local drivers from trying. The basic requirements are one foot hard on the accelerator and one hand permanently depressing the horn to clear a path through the hordes of cyclists, often loaded down with bags of rice or other produce — not to mention whole families — ox-carts, locally-made tractors (built at low cost for durability not speed or looks) and pedestrians reluctant to surrender the space they have gained.

At some stage, usually every few yards, one is confronted by an onrushing truck or passenger bus, both invariably heavily overloaded and leaning over at an alarming angle, which requires fine judgement in giving way at the last possible second to avoid a collision by inches. The wrecks littering the roadside attest to the fact that good judgement is not always present.

Vietnamese residents of Ho Chi Minh City warn that there has been an increase in street crime. The streets of Dong Khoi, Nguyen Hue, Le Loi, as well as areas in front of major hotels including Saigon Floating and New World, where many foreigners circulate, are favourite spots for pickpockets, other thieves and muggers, usually operating from motorbikes.

In the latter category, a motorcycle swoops down on an unwary pedestrian at the roadside. The pillion passenger snatches a briefcase or handbag (some of the best can also strip a watch off a wrist in a twinkling) and the motorcycle disappears into the traffic at high speed.

Foreigners in particular are warned to be very careful about walking alone in the streets at night, even in well-lit city centres. Especially at night is it inadvisable to travel by cyclo. Some visitors have been harrassed, forced to pay two to three times the agreed fare on reaching their destination, and sometimes mugged, after taking what they thought would be a relaxed way of seeing the city.

Hanoi

Petty street crime such as bag or necklace-snatching are also on the rise in Hanoi, which was 'crime-free' until 1994. Pickpocketing on buses has become a major problem as more people commute to town. When it comes to witnessing thieves in action, Vietnamese in Hanoi and Ho Chi Minh City apparently turn a blind eye, as it is none of their business, regarding crime as a social problem that 'society' (i.e. the government) should solve.

Begging is common in the cities and countryside, and sometimes it can be very persistent. In the south, the beggars tend to be war invalids, some of them with hideous reminders of the conflict.

Top Tip: Beware of Beggars

Swarms of small children tend to surround foreigners whether walking on the streets or sitting at an open-air cafe or food-stall. They will look so forlorn that it is tempting to give them money. But it should be remembered that many of these children work for adult syndicates who will pocket most of the cash. Begging may be merely an excuse for a robbery attempt.

Another juvenile pest is the shoeshine boy, who seems to be everywhere in the country eager to polish those dusty-looking shoes. They can be very persistent. Should you decide to succumb, payment should not exceed 4,000 dong, or say 20 pence or 30 US cents.

6

Food & Drink

Baguettes

Vietnamese cooking, while possessing a unique style all its own, has also been heavily influenced over the centuries mainly by China, Cambodia and other Southeast Asian nations. Stir-frying, deep frying and even chopsticks, for example, were introduced from China about a thousand years ago and became firmly embedded in northern culinary culture at least. The southern part of the country has been influenced more by Cambodia, Thailand and India. But although the ingredients may be appear to be the same, southern Vietnamese food is more subtle and less overwhelmingly spicy.

Items like bamboo shoots, bean-curd, lotus roots or nuts, bean sprouts, chives, Chinese cabbage, water spinach and kale will be familiar to anyone who has travelled in Asia before. Vietnamese cooking, however, depends heavily on a wide range of fresh herbs to provide distinctive flavours which locals insist mark the cuisine out as separate from any other.

Vietnamese restaurants around the country range from the tiny, street-side *pho* stalls, offering a noodle-based soup which is standard fare for many Vietnamese, especially in the north, to full-blown, opulent operations targeting foreign visitors and well-heeled Vietnamese.

The soup in *pho* is normally made from oxtail or beef stock, lavishly seasoned with a variety of spices and herbs, including crushed chillies, ginger, cinnamon and star of anise. In the north, thin strips of raw beef are likely to be added.

Many hotels and restaurants specialize in providing a comprehensive, banquet-style meal, specifically aimed at tourists wishing to sample different foods from around the country under what might be delicately called 'controlled conditions'. Other restaurants cater to a more select clientele offering perhaps one or two specialities, but at a price.

Top Tip: Bread & Coffee French-style

The French occupation provides a legacy of wonderful fresh-baked bread. An excellent cheap and satisfying meal, for example, is a fresh baguette filled with salad, local paté, cheese, or, especially at breakfast time, just butter and jam. Even in the smallest towns and villages one can find vendors selling crispy bread rolls filled with ground pork with herbal seasoning.

A fondness for coffee is also apparent throughout the country, small cups of *cafe filtre* being especially popular in the south.

The more adventurous visitor, however, can plunge into the back streets of Hanoi and Ho Chi Minh City to discover hole-in-the-wall establishments that offer authentic cuisine at low prices. Language may prove a problem in such places, but pointing at what one's fellow diners are having is a good substitute. However, as fresh, raw vegetables are very popular in many Vietnamese dishes, in some of the less well-appointed eating establishments it would be well to ensure that these ingredients have been thoroughly washed.

Anyone familiar with Chinese takeaways will relish the Vietnamese spring rolls (*nem* in the north and *cha gio* in the south) filled with shrimps, vermicelli, chopped onion and mushroom, which tend to be thinner and more delicate than their Chinese counterparts.

Many sauces are provided with most meals, including soy sauce and chilli sauce. There is also the ubiquitous *nuoc mam*, which can best be

Vietnamese dishes

described as 'rotten fish sauce' and a bit discouraging for the first-time visitor.

*N*uoc *mam* is indeed a fish-based sauce, unique to Vietnam and considered as essential accompaniment to most meals. It is prepared from various species of fish that are mixed with salt and then left to liquefy in wooden barrels for several months – the longer the brewing period the finer the sauce and the higher its price. It can be used alone as a dip, or mixed with garlic, chilli, sugar, vinegar and fresh lime, when it is known as *nuoc cham*.

Among meats, pork and chicken dishes are the most plentiful because both animals are bred in large quantities (unlike beef, which tends to be expensive for this reason). The best way to eat these is to find a restaurant where one can barbecue the meat over a charcoal burner, adding to taste from a vast plateful of herbs and vegetables invariably provided – comprising items such as lettuce, onion, mint, basil, parsley, plus an assortment of fiery red and green peppers – and then dipped in *nuoc mam*.

Western visitors accustomed to eating only chicken breasts, however, should be warned that in Vietnam, like China, one tends to get everything – bone, gristle and various internal organs of a dubious nature. In fact, some of the bits Westerners might normally discard, such as the feet, are highly-prized delicacies and at a banquet are usually given to the guest of honour as a mark of respect.

Especially popular in the northern winter is what is known elsewhere in the region by such names as 'steamboat' and 'Mongolian hotpot' and here called *lan*. A large bowl, filled with seasoned broth, is placed on charcoal brazier with meat and vegetables added by the cook or by each individual diner. Apart from meat, fish is also used and one of the best dishes of the latter type is known as *cha ca*.

Given Vietnam's long coastline, of course, fresh fish is plentiful and cheap. The giant prawns, cuttlefish and crabs are delicious, even more so if they can be selected live from a tank within the restaurant. Eels are also popular.

There is plenty of choice over what to drink with the meal. Locally brewed beers, often major brands produced under licence in Vietnam, abound. There are also domestic brands, the best known in the south being 333, whose notoriously heavy use of formaldehyde can result in a pretty nasty hangover. In the north, Halida is the most frequently drunk brand. *Bia hoi* or fresh beer is worth sampling in major cities. Wine is available in major urban centres and tends to come from France or Australia.

There are also some potent local liquors, notably a rice wine called *ruou de*, which is similar to Japanese sake and has the same lethal effect on the legs unless approached with caution.

Top Tip: Water Watch

Although it's just about safe to brush your teeth in tap water, it is not wise to drink it. In a restaurant play safe and order bottled water. This can be especially important during the country's regular floods, when the water is most susceptible to contamination. Ice is normally produced from purified water, but it is always best to check in advance with the establishment serving it. If there is even the slightest doubt play safe and drink your whiskey and water warm.

Drinking water provided by hotels is boiled and should be safe, but, again, it may be wiser to buy bottled purified or mineral water. The most popular of the latter is *La Vie*, drawn from a natural spring some 60 kilometres from Ho Chi Minh City by a Franco-Vietnamese joint venture. However, be careful when buying as many local imitators have sprung up using almost identical bottle shapes and labels to try and confuse the consumer.

When dining out, it should be noted that some restaurants charge an extra five to 10 per cent for payment by credit card. Tipping, however, is not usually encouraged, although some hotel restaurants add a service charge. Restaurant bills are also subject to government tax.

Eating out is a way of life, although more so in the south than the north. With many wives working these days, and homes tending to be somewhat small for handling visitors, foreign visitors invited to dine by Vietnamese friends or business associates tend to find this means eating in a public place.

It makes sense to form a large party in order to enjoy a Vietnamese meal to the full. The idea is that a large number of varied dishes, reflecting a full range of tastes and textures and cooking techniques, should be ordered and placed in the middle of the table for communal dining. Westerners who would normally expect to eat their food along with a bowl of rice, as happens in Japan for instance, will find that Vietnam normally follows the Chinese custom of serving rice at the end of the meal. But it is possible to ask for it to be served earlier in the meal.

7

Shopping

Streetside eating

When Saigon, the former capital of US-backed South Vietnam, fell in 1975, the new rulers vowed to transform what they saw as a 'reactionary and rotten' city into a sober bastion of socialism. To underscore their intent, they renamed the city in memory of their deceased revolutionary leader Ho Chi Minh.

But any foreigner with personal experience of earlier times in Vietnam returning today to Ho Chi Minh City will have little trouble adapting.

Commerce still courses through the city's veins. Smuggled television sets from Japan, pirated compact discs from China, fake Levi jeans from Thailand – everything is on offer in a city parts of which look increasingly like Bangkok.

It is said America shipped an average 2,000 tonnes of equipment to Vietnam every day of the war. Much of it was left behind when the last helicopters fled on 30 April 1975, and can be found in backstreet shops and underground markets. Down by the Saigon River in a line of shacks known simply as American Market one could equip an army with dog-tags, night-scopes, boots, flak jackets and even parachutes. On Dong Khoi Street or in Dan Sinh Market in the tourist district, dozens of shops get by selling GI pens, cigarette lighters and dead men's sunglasses.

Mini-helicopters made out of Coca-Cola cans and 'Good Morning Vietnam' T-shirts are brisk sellers on market stalls alongside supposed GI dog-tags which baby-faced vendors insist date from two decades ago. Most will want payment in 'greenbacks' – the dollar being the currency of preference.

Out in the Chinese district of Cholon, the business ethic rules supreme as it has always done. Areas tend to have their own product specialities which can easily be assessed as they lie piled up on the pavement outside the narrow shophouses that always seem to be jostling for air.

After years of drab, Soviet-bloc-standard consumer durables, Vietnamese are looking for a change and keeping their eye open for quality. This tends to result in American products being number one, European number two and Asian countries, number three, except in automobiles/transportation where Japan is number one.

Denim jeans, perhaps the ultimate casual Western fashion statement of all, are now officially made in Vietnam. Though bogus versions of Levi's and Calvin Klein jeans have been sold here for years, a Singaporean joint venture is now manufacturing the goods locally. Since 1994, a number of Western clothes shops have opened in Ho Chi Minh City. Their products are not cheap.

Purchasing power is also boosted by the fact that most Vietnamese own their own houses, usually do not take holidays, do not pay for superannuation and have hardly any tax or insurance payments to fulfil. In addition, the majority live as extended families – average households contain six persons – where income is pooled for major purchases.

But companies hoping to make their mark have to keep in mind Vietnam's cultural, historical, geographical and religious differences which have different influences than those of modern Western markets. Since Hanoians have less money to spend, they still tend to purchase cheaper, but essential consumer goods, while Saigonese are already beginning to purchase 'big ticket' items such as motorcycles, cars and cellular phones.

One of the most noticeable differences between Hanoians and Saigonese consumers is their perception of advertisements. For example, if a television commercial is not directly product-related, the Saigonese tend to dismiss it, saying: 'What does this commercial have to do with the product?' Any unrealistic portrayal of a product will raise doubts as to the sincerity and quality of the market and thus jeopardize its marketability.

In contrast, Hanoians seem to enjoy television commercials for their sheer entertainment value. This could be due to the poor variety of entertainment available in the North. So long as a commercial does not attack their family values, the commercial will be seen on the whole as suitable.

Cham sculpture, Da Nang

The presence of the French and then the Americans played a significant role in altering

Southern Vietnamese desires, expectations and purchasing habits. Branding of product names into the consciousness of the Saigonese seems to have achieved much greater penetration than in Hanoi. Saigonese are aware of branding and have already made the association of brand name with high quality – such as having a Sony or Honda Dream II motorcycle. As a whole, Saigonese have more exposure to foreign products than the rest of the country.

The North has only just begun to understand branding. For example, they identify a Sony product with top quality but are still largely unaware of other brand names. Today, branding in Vietnam is not so much a question of purchasing a product because of its name or manufacturer but rather where the products come from, as already noted.

Hanoians still predominantly shop in markets, largely because those involved in agriculture continue to represent well over 40 per cent of Hanoi's work-force, whereas only about 14 per cent of Saigonese work on the land. With the influx of mini-marts and bigger state-run shopping centres, southerners are getting more and more exposure to new products and choices for the moment.

In the capital, a memorable shopping expedition involves wandering through a labyrinth of narrow streets in the old part of the city, unchanged for many decades, where traditional trades were carried out, each in a designated area still identified by the names of the thoroughfares – Silk Street, Gold Street etc. Now, the predominant image is of masses of small shop houses, bulging with goods spilling out onto the pavement, primarily clothing of every description, electrical products, medicines and traditional arts. The streets are thronged from morning to night with a vast press of pedestrians, making movement by any form of motor vehicle extremely difficult. In the maze of look-alike streets running off at all angles, it is easy to imagine getting lost.

Top Tip: Take Your 'Essentials' with You!

For the foreign visitor, the shopping experience can vary. Some of the items one is accustomed to finding in the corner-shop back home may not be available, or, if they are, prohibitively expensive. Short-term visitors should plan to be self-sufficient in the basic essentials, while those planning longer stays tend to stock up on items in short supply during visits to neighbouring shopping paradises like Singapore, Hong Kong and Bangkok.

The Vietnamese excel in various arts. Lacquerware, ceramics, fine embroidery, traditional silk painting and woodblock prints are all items worth taking back home. Rattan furniture is cheap, although it is more likely to be bought by long-term residents rather than tourists. For the latter, Vietnam has an abundance of precious stones which can be turned into jewellery quickly and relatively cheaply.

Antiques are everywhere, but the visitor buying such items can run into problems when trying to export them. The law says no antiques may be taken out of the country, but it is rather ambiguous on classification of what constitutes a protected item. Therefore, it is best to check before buying.

Top Tip: Bargaining Business

In general, whenever an exchange of money for a good or service takes place, bargaining is the essential means of settling the price – although a fixed price system is beginning to emerge in areas frequented by tourists.

The Vietnamese are extremely tough bargainers and, with a vast fund of patience, it is very difficult for a foreigner to come anywhere near winning the game. If time is not a problem, it pays to shop around, and always be prepared to walk away if the bargaining process is not getting anywhere.

8

Business Tips

Antiques shop, Xha San

There is a general consensus that in seeking to do business with and/or in Vietnam, much stress and frustration, as they say, come with the territory. Above all, everyone – and that includes the Vietnamese side – has to learn to wait, to be patient. As was demonstrated in the Vietnam War, the Vietnamese are a people who can wait and wait to get a deal that is most advantageous to them. Westerners tend to expect action 'now'. This can lead to business deals being scrapped because the foreign side has lost patience in the protracted nature of the negotiations.

Sometimes, it seems as if the Vietnamese feel they have to behave this way in order to show their toughness and business acumen, especially given their limited experience in the international business arena.

Top Tip: Understand Confucianism

To understand Vietnam's business culture, one must first consider the culture of the country. Confucianism still permeates much of Vietnamese life in some form or other, and in business that can often mean extremely bright, go-ahead young business executives forced to show deference to the boss, who may have reached his position by patiently waiting for the years to accumulate rather than through the demonstration of any special talent.

Vietnam for years followed a socialist model designed by the former Soviet Union, and this still tends to exert some influence. The result has been a business culture characterized by extreme caution with drawn-out decision-making process.

The demise of socialism in Eastern Europe as a commercial model and the switch to the market economy has resulted in a kind of split personality; some managers cling to socialist practices while others energetically forge ahead. Also, there is now emerging a young entrepreneurial class whose methods are firmly rooted in the capitalist system. This group is often self-assertive and aggressive, and is predominantly concerned with short-term goals rather than long-term growth.

Given the strong sense of national pride and independence, foreign business people sometimes complain that their Vietnamese counterparts are suspicious and tough to deal with. This is not simply a result of centuries of foreign involvement, but also of the influence of Asian business practices where relationships are important precursors to business negotiations.

Since Vietnam has only recently opened its doors to the outside world, it is too early to make concrete predictions about the direction its business culture will take. However, Vietnam's Latinized alphabet and fascination with the West sets the stage for a migration towards Western business practices. The country has a remarkable ability to absorb foreign influence while retaining its character and the people are pragmatic – using what works and discarding what doesn't.

Top Tip: Don't Worry About Gift-giving

Business rituals in Vietnam are much the same as anywhere else, so that a basic combination of politeness and common-sense should see the business executive through a negotiating process without serious etiquette difficulties. Vietnamese business meetings tend to be relaxed affairs with less of the formality that one encounters particularly in Japan and to a lesser extent in China. Exchanges of gifts common in China do not seem to be part of the Vietnamese culture.

Meetings are an integral part of doing business in Vietnam, face-to-face contact being considered vital; few, if any, negotiations are possible by phone, fax or letter. Businessmen with a lot of experience on the ground warn that meetings tend to take a lot longer than you might anticipate, so it is not considered wise to fill the day with too many tight appointments, some of which might eventually have to be cancelled amid much embarrassment.

Shoe stall, near Long Bien Bridge

Business cards should be exchanged with everyone in the room on the initial encounter before any discussions have taken place. But unlike Japan, it is not necessary to be terribly formal (i.e. handing over the card with two hands accompanied by a deep bow). But politeness suggests you pause briefly to examine the card and then wait for the opposite principal to sit down before doing so yourself.

Tea-drinking is an essential business ritual as in other parts of Asia. Again, it is usually considered polite to wait for the senior member on the other side to begin drinking before doing so oneself. A few sips will be quite sufficient for politeness' sake, especially if you don't find the tea to your liking. You may be offered a cigarette, and although smoking is prevalent in Vietnam it is not obligatory to light up and a polite refusal will not be taken amiss!

Good communication is obviously of paramount importance. For a long-term commitment, it would be advisable to learn the language. If, however, you are forced to use a translator, in conversation always face the person you are addressing and try not to talk to the interpreter all the time.

It is considered a good idea to let your Vietnamese counterpart speak uninterruptedly for a stretch. The advice is not to question him or her immediately on points you think ought to be dealt with there and then. It is far more polite, and effective, to make notes, bringing up queries when it is your turn to speak.

One can be direct, without being *too* firm, even though the other side may not be. There may be many reasons why your Vietnamese counterpart cannot give a straight answer – including the need to check with his or her political masters – other than sheer negotiating deviousness.

Top Tip: Be Prepared for Serious Drinking

Entertaining is, as elsewhere in Asia, an important part of the business ritual, although it may not necessarily occur at the first encounter. However, at some stage, an opportunity will arrive to unwind and get to know each other better. Vietnamese banquets can be fairly riotous affairs, with a great deal of drinking, so it helps to have a strong head and stomach. It starts to get serious when the words *tram phan tram* (100 per cent) are spoken, indicating that you are being urged to down the entire contents of the glass at one go. Anyone with experience of the Chinese *'gambei'* (bottoms up) will know what this entails!

9

Social Situations

Reunification Hall, Memorial to Ho Chi Minh

The Vietnamese are a proud, independent-minded people. It is therefore very important to avoid situations where one might be suspected of displaying an outdated 'colonial attitude'. This could involve saying something that sounds condescending. Likewise with one's actions.

Vietnamese place a great emphasis on creating and maintaining social harmony. Thus, they may avoid unpleasant topics or tell 'white lies' in order to defuse a potentially embarrassing situation. It is often very difficult to get a direct 'yes-no' answer out of them. For this reason, the foreign visitor may find it difficult to understand when he or she has done something that is considered in some way inappropriate or even unacceptable. Then one has to become something of an amateur psychologist to look for clues in uncomfortable silences or lack of eye contact.

Speaking of direct eye contact, this is usually avoided in many social situations until the two sides know each other well. A Western man who stared at a pretty young girl would find her bashfully looking away, or perhaps even feeling indignant at this violation of all known rules.

Modesty is considered a great social virtue. Hence, Vietnamese will invariably speak in the most modest, self-deprecatory terms about themselves.

Age is vitally important because increasing seniority in years brings with it honour and respect. Therefore, in meeting a group of Vietna-

---

Top Tip: Watch Your Voice Level!

Raising one's voice or becoming angry is considered a sign that one lacks self-discipline. It all creates a highly embarrassing situation for the person being shouted at and should be avoided.

Vietnamese, like other peoples in Asia, place great stress on saving 'face'. They are very skilled in detecting the real attitudes of others through tone of voice and body language and react accordingly.

mese for the first time, it is important to pay attention to the 'pecking order' and seek to greet people according to their rank within the group, whether it be a business enterprise or a family.

Many Westerners are tactile by nature, but this can get them into trouble in a conservative society like Vietnam. It is considered highly impolite to touch anyone of the opposite sex, no matter how innocent the motive – even a little pat of encouragement. It is rare, therefore, to see even a married couple holding hands in public (although the more 'Westernized' younger generation in the big cities sometimes flout this convention).

Temple of Literature, Hanoi

However, physical contact between the same sex is considered quite acceptable as a token of friendship. But as many people believe that a spirit lives in the head and shoulders, these are two areas of the body best avoided.

Although, as we have seen, the Vietnamese often avoid giving a straight answer, that does not stop them asking foreigners very direct questions about their age, marital status, family background, and even how much the clothes cost that they are wearing. This stems from a natural curiosity about life outside their country which few of them have had or will have a chance to see. One has a choice of answering frankly, or turning the questions aside in a gentle, joking manner that will not cause offence.

It may take a little time to cultivate the sort of friendships that bring about an invitation to visit a Vietnamese family home. Depending on political, economic and social status, that home may be rather simple and cramped, with very limited privacy, which is why many Vietnamese prefer to take their foreign friends to a restaurant for a meal instead.

If one is invited home, however, take a small present, but do not expect to see it opened while you are on the premises. Unless the friendship is very close, it would be unwise to drop in on a family uninvited, thus causing embarrassment that the house is not tidy enough to receive visitors. Normally, it is not wise to make casual calls around lunchtime, as it is traditional for everyone to enjoy a small siesta after the meal.

Immediately on entering the house, the guest automatically will be served a drink, usually tea or perhaps fruit juice. One is not obligated to drink it beyond a few sips – an empty cup or glass usually obliges the host to fill it up again!

Top Tip: Dangerous Liaisons!

Romantic partnerships between locals and foreigners are not actively encouraged, but they do occur. But a Westerner should be aware that casual liaisons are frowned upon, and that one should not start a romance without the most serious intentions. A chaperone may well be considered appropriate for the couple in the early days of their courting.

If a relationship is permitted to develop and then sours, face may be lost on the Vietnamese side which will create a difficult situation for the foreigner involved when an angry family comes a-calling.

10

Useful Words & Phrases

Tai Chi

Vietnamese began life as a mixture of Thai, Khmer and Muong languages, but was then heavily influenced by China which provided the bulk of the vocabulary. From the 9th to the 16th centuries, the Chinese script was used for writing. But then, with the influx of French Catholic missionaries, a romanized version emerged called Quoc Ngu which finally became official in 1920. Not surprisingly, pronunciation is based on the French alphabet.

Like Chinese, it is a heavily tonal language, creating all sorts of possibilities for the hapless foreigner to mispronounce a word and thus change its meaning, to the delight of the natives. There are six tones in the north and five in the south, and a simple word like *ma* can, for example mean horse, mother, ghost, rice seedling or tomb, depending on the way it is said. (Do try the words and expressions listed below. Your efforts will be much appreciated. However, because there is no easy guide to pronunciation, it is better to learn as you go, with help from your, no doubt, admiring hosts!)

To add to the potential confusion, social custom also dictates different words to be used when greeting someone, depending on their age, sex and status, although the stumbling foreigner will almost certainly be forgiven any linguistic indiscretion. The various greetings are:

chào ông	to an older or important man (grandfather).
chào anh	to a younger man (brother, husband).
chào chú	to a man younger than your father but older than you (uncle).
chào bà	to an old or important woman (grandmother).
chào chị	to an older woman (sister).
chào cô	to a younger woman (aunt)
chào em	to a child, male or female; someone subordinate to you; or someone close, such as a husband or very good friend.
chào bạn	to a friend of your age.

Useful words

Thank you	**Cám ởn.** The other person may reply **Không có chi** (You are welcome)
Hello	**Xin chào**
Goodbye	**Tạm biệt**
Excuse me	**Tôi xin lỗi**
I am very pleased to meet you	**Tôi rất hân hạnh dưởc gặp anh**
Yes	**Phải**
No	**Không**
What is this?	**Dây là cá gì** (for an object)
Who is this?	**Dây là ai?**
I don't know	**Tôi không biết**
I don't understand	**Tôi không hiểu**
Maybe	**Có thể**
That's okay/no problem	**Không sao**
Please	**Vui lòng**
Already	**Xong rồi**
Where is the bathroom?	**Câu tiêu ở đâu?**
Go	**Đi đi** (used to brush off beggars or people bothering you)
bus station	**bến xe**
taxi	**xe tắc xi**
cyclo	**xe xích lô**
train	**xe lửả**
where is . . .?	**ở đâu . . .?**
motorbike taxi	**hon đa ôm**
turn right	**quẹo phải**
turn left	**quẹo trái**
stop	**dửng lại**

Numbers

zero	không
one	một
two	hai
three	ba
four	bốn
five	năm
six	saú
seven	bảy
eight	tám
nine	chiń
ten	mười
eleven	mười một
twenty	hai mười
twenty one	hai mười một

Facts About Vietnam

Vietnam is an elongated 'S'-shaped country, 1,650 kilometres long and only 50 kilometres wide at its narrowest point. Covering almost 15 degrees of latitude, it goes from a tropical climate of perpetual summer in the south to a far north where freezing winters are not unknown.

Vietnam has a current population of some 72 million, of whom about 10 per cent live in two main urban areas, Hanoi and Ho Chi Minh City.

In 1996, the Vietnamese unemployment rate in the big cities was around seven per cent – about 2.6 million people – rising to nearly 40 per cent, or some six million people, in the countryside. The workforce numbers 29.5 million in the countryside and 9.2 million in the cities.

The Vietnam War resulted in an estimated one million military and another 1.5 million civilian dead. Sixty per cent of southern villages were destroyed; in the north every major town and provincial capital, along with main roads, railway lines, bridges, ports and industrial facilities were repeatedly bombed. Fifteen million people were rendered homeless throughout the country.

The Vietnamese declaration of independence drawn up by President Ho Chi Minh in 1945 is modelled on, and its preamble matches the language of, the American version.

In his younger days, President Ho Chi Minh briefly worked as a hotel cook in England.

The ethnic breakdown is Vietnamese (86.8 per cent), minorities (10 per cent), Chinese (1.5 per cent), Khmer (1.4 per cent).

Taiwan is the largest industrial foreign investor, followed by Japan, although the United States is catching up fast after a late start due to diplomatic relations between the two countries only being established in 1995.

Vietnam's chief exports are crude oil, minerals and coal (30 per cent), rice, rubber, other agricultural products and marine products (50 per cent), manufactured goods, mainly textiles (20 per cent).

The most popular family name, occurring almost 50 per cent of the time, is Nguyen, the title of the final imperial dynasty. The family name is normally placed first, followed by the given names.

WAR MEMORIES

About 40 miles northwest of Ho Chi Minh City, the reconstructed Cu Chi tunnel complex offers tourists a chance to crawl through the labyrinthine, claustrophobic network to experience the life of the Viet Cong guerrillas who hid there from incessant B-52 bombing raids during the Vietnam War. Similar tunnels have been opened up to tourism in Vinh Moe, Quang Tri Province, near the former Demilitarized Zone between North and South. There is even a firing range, at $1 per live round.

Parts of the Ho Chi Minh Trail – the legendary wartime jungle logistics route along the Laos and Cambodian border by which the North fed its war machine in the South – may be turned into a tourist attraction.

When the film *Indochine* starring Catherine Deneuve was shown in cinemas in her native France, it is said that the number of French tourists to Vietnam doubled in three months. For a modest $100 a night one can even stay in the suite she used at the Ha Long Bay Hotel in northern Vietnam during several weeks of shooting in the area – although the waiting list is a long one.

Vietnamese women after marriage continue to use their own name, rather than adopting that of their husband. There is also no distinction in the language between Mrs and Miss. Children, however, take their father's family name.

Some superstitions in Vietnam are opposite to those in the West. Thus, a black cat straying across your path or into your house would be considered unlucky. However, a dog brings good luck. To dream of a dead person or a fire is also considered as a portent of good luck. White is prime mourning colour not black.

Dancing was banned after the Vietnam War until 1986, but both the ballroom and disco versions have become popular once again. Karaoke is very popular.

Climate

Vietnam is a tropical country, with a monsoon climate, and high humidity. However, the country can be divided into two climatic regions – the central and southern region has very warm, humid weather throughout the year, while the northern region has a distinct winter season (October to February) with temperatures around 5-10 degrees C and a very hot summer season (May to July) when temperatures average 28-37 degrees C. Rainfall varies between an annual average 150cm in the plains to 200-300cm in the mountains.

Vietnam uses the Metric system of weights and measures; electricity supply is 220V AC, and traffic drives on the right.

The Vietnamese currency is the Dong (VND). There are 100VND, 200VND, 500VND, 1000VND, 10000VND, 20000VND and 50000VND notes.

Officially, tipping is not permitted but in practice it is still widespread.

Banks are open from 8.00a.m.-4.30p.m. Monday-Friday and from 8.00a.m.-12.00 noon on Saturday. Office hours are 7.30a.m.-4.30p.m. Monday-Saturday, but they close 12.00 noon-1.00p.m. Shops are open 7.30a.m.-12.00 noon and 1.00p.m.-4.30p.m. every day including Sunday.

Emergency phone numbers: Fire 15, Medical Assistance 14.

Index

SOMERSET MURDER STORIES

RECALLING THE EVENTS OF SOME OF SOMERSET AND BRISTOL'S
MOST WELL-KNOWN MURDERS

Neil Walden

BRADWELL
BOOKS

Published by Bradwell Books

11 Orgreave Close Sheffield S13 9NP

Email: books@bradwellbooks.co.uk

British Library Cataloguing in Publication Data: a catalogue record for this book is available from the British Library.

1st Edition

ISBN: 9781912060603

Design by: Andrew Caffrey

Typesetting by: Mark Titterton

Photograph credits: The author, Creative Commons (CC) and indicated separately

Print: Gomer Press, Llandysul, Ceredigion SA44 4JL

ACKNOWLEDGEMENTS

I would particularly like to thank The Soldiers of Gloucestershire Museum for their help with providing further details relating to service records and also to Bill Walden for providing the drawings of Hinks and Parrington Jackson.

CONTENTS

INTRODUCTION

IN THIS BOOK OF TRUE MURDER STORIES FROM AROUND
SOMERSET AND BRISTOL YOU WILL SEE THAT I HAVE
COVERED THE PERIOD FROM THE 1840S TO THE 1940S. WHILE
CONCENTRATING ON THIS PARTICULAR ERA I FOUND THAT
THERE WERE MANY FASCINATING CRIMES TO CHOOSE FROM.
I HAVE TRIED TO SELECT THE MURDER CASES THAT HAVE
INTERESTING STORIES ASSOCIATED WITH THEM, RATHER
THAN RELATING ANY WHICH ARE SIMPLY RANDOM ACTS OF
BRUTALITY.

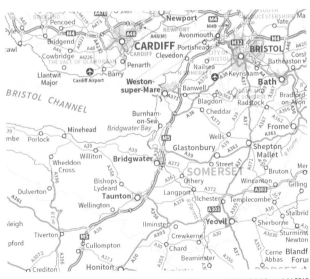

Ordnance Survey data © Crown copyright and database right 2018

The title of each of the chapters is taken from the contemporary newspaper reports of the crimes. Among these cases you will find several stories which are seldom recounted in books of this nature. These are mixed in with others that were huge news stories in their own time, such as the cases of Amelia Dyer and George Smith. In these instances, with the central facts widely known, I have tried to focus on the particular links to our region.

All the stories come from a time when the death penalty was still in place. Yet, of the sixteen murder cases related in these pages, just nine of the murderers were sent to the scaffold. Some of the killers were given surprisingly lenient sentences while others were simply never apprehended.

The Bristol Station Murder

ON 15 OCTOBER 1917, ON PLATFORM FIVE OF BRISTOL TEMPLE MEADS STATION, BESSIE CROSS WAS SHOT DEAD. THERE WAS NEVER ANY QUESTION THAT HER HUSBAND ALBERT WAS RESPONSIBLE BUT, IN A VERDICT THAT FLEW IN THE FACE OF ALL THE KNOWN FACTS, WHEN HE WAS TRIED HE WAS FOUND TO BE NOT GUILTY OF HER MURDER.

At the start of the First World War Bessie and Albert Cross were living in Lower Guinea Street with their two sons, Harry and Edwin. Albert had been working as a painter but volunteered almost immediately when war was declared and was serving with the Second Gloucester Regiment on the Western Front. By the summer of 1917 Bessie, now 27 years old, had moved to 9 Henry Row, Baptist Mills in Bristol. To make ends meet she had rented out the front two rooms of the house to Elizabeth Parry. Like Bessie, Elizabeth was alone as her husband Walter was also away fighting.

During this period, it seems another visitor to Henry Row was James King, who was a fitter's labourer. Soon Bessie became pregnant by King, but it seems that it

Bristol Temple Meads railway station, where on 15 October 1917
Albert Cross murdered his wife

was King who was the one to break the news to her husband. Albert received King's letter in the trenches, informing him that Bessie was pregnant but that it was over between them. Albert was clearly distraught and on 28 August he sent his reply to King.

Naturally the letter is full of anger, but also of contradictions as he sways between one emotion and another. He admonishes King for hunting down women whose husbands are away fighting and at one point he states that he lives only for Bessie and the children and that he considers King to be a coward. He also adds that if King has any family of his own then he is equally sorry for them, especially his wife. In fact, King did indeed have a long-suffering wife, Martha, as well as six children.

There were also anguished letters between Albert and Bessie which were sent in the period leading up to Albert's return to Bristol on leave. The first night of Albert's visit, which was 5 October 1917, was inevitably a miserable affair as he and Bessie tried to find a way through the predicament. Elizabeth, the lodger, could not help hearing Bessie and Albert arguing deep into the night, with Albert becoming so agitated that he walked out, heading towards Victoria Street to sleep at the servicemen's club. Bessie followed and the two of them returned ten minutes later, only for the arguments to continue until the morning.

After this terrible first night the situation did seem to improve and the remainder of the stay passed reasonably amicably, right up until they left for Albert to rejoin his regiment. It seemed to people who met them that Albert had found it in his heart to forgive his wife. Clearly it was not that simple.

Witnesses at Temple Meads claim that they heard Bessie's scream moments before he shot her. They reported that Bessie had her hands raised and was facing Albert as he raised the rifle to his waist, pointing the gun into her abdomen before pulling the trigger.

Bessie was taken by ambulance to the General Hospital where, in the operating theatre, the situation was found to be hopeless and she died soon after. The post-mortem revealed a wound to the right side of Bessie's abdomen.

The bullet had split in transit through her body, something which would have added to the internal damage.

The nearest witnesses to the incident were two soldiers on the platform. As they had approached Albert, he stated, 'I have shot my wife.' A foreman for Midland Railways took the gun while Albert remained perfectly calm as he explained that his wife was pregnant by another man. Albert Cross was taken to Bedminster police station and charged with the murder of his wife.

The coroner's jury were to return a verdict of wilful murder against Albert but it was King's behaviour rather than Albert's that caused most disgust. The coroner described King's letter to Albert while he was away at the front as the most dastardly act that could possibly be imagined. Speaking directly to King, he added, 'There was only one man responsible for that woman's death and that man is you.' Nevertheless, the date was set for Albert's trial.

The current mood in the country must have given Albert slight grounds for optimism. There was a groundswell of patriotism at the time of the inquest, which coincided with Trafalgar Day. In Bristol crowds were gathering at the tramway centre to watch the brave soldiers come to the city to attend the various receptions and events staged to commemorate those who had fought for their country.

By the time of the trial it seemed that everyone was content to treat the whole incident as if it had been a tragic accident. It reached its conclusion with the judge inviting the jury to find the verdict in favour of Albert Cross, saying, 'Do not judge a man used to the grim side of war as if they were an ordinary prisoner.' With these words ringing in their ears the jury acquitted Albert after just ninety minutes of deliberation.

The headlines of the newspapers of 25 November referred to 'The Unwritten Law', presumably condoning an act of revenge against those who are disloyal while the troops are away fighting. They were clearly delighted with the verdict of not guilty. Surely this was a verdict that could only have been reached at a time when the country was on a war footing: on one hand the soldier who was fighting for his country so bravely and on the other a man perceived to be lurking in the safety of Bristol and failing to do his duty.

With Albert exonerated he was released to rejoin his regiment. He was soon part of the savage action of Operation Michael, the German offensive to capture the Channel ports. On the second day of the battle of St Quentin, among the carnage, thick fog and confusion he was taken captive as a prisoner of war. After the hostilities were finally over he came back to Bristol and by the close of 1919 he was married to his new wife, Ada. The army life obviously suited Albert and he stayed in the forces until he was finally discharged in 1924.

The Rode Murder

DURING THE NIGHT OF 29 JUNE 1860, THREE-YEAR-OLD FRANCIS SAVILLE KENT DISAPPEARED FROM HIS BEDROOM AT ROAD HILL HOUSE, IN THE VILLAGE OF RODE, EAST SOMERSET, CLOSE TO THE WILTSHIRE BORDER. THE NEXT MORNING, AFTER A DESPERATE SEARCH, THE YOUNG BOY WAS FOUND IN THE OUTSIDE TOILET WITH HIS THROAT CUT.

The case has many of the elements of a classic country house mystery and that is mainly because these events are, to a large extent, responsible for the development of that particular style of fiction. The writers of the time read the case as it unfolded in the newspapers and it fired their imaginations to create stories that often had more than a passing resemblance to the case.

The gallery of suspects included three live-in servants and half a dozen other domestic staff who were employed by Samuel Saville Kent to look after his rather dysfunctional family. Kent himself had caused a lot of disharmony in the household by marrying a woman twenty years his junior, who had been the children's governess, just months after the death of his first wife.

The police investigations into the murder of the young child were initially hindered by the involvement of both the Wiltshire and Somerset police forces. It seems that both time and important evidence were lost in the crucial early period. Some forensic evidence was seemingly deliberately overlooked to avoid bringing distress to the family and it does seem that the local police were more anxious to find a culprit from among the poorer villagers than the comparatively wealthy Kent family. In mid-July Detective Inspector Jack Whicher arrived from Scotland Yard and immediately the case was examined afresh with a new degree of professionalism.

While rumours and suspicion had swirled around Samuel (for example, one theory was that the young boy had been killed as part of an insurance fraud) it was the victim's nursemaid, Elizabeth Gough, who was bearing the brunt of the suspicion and had been arrested. An early police theory was that Gough had been with a man in her bedroom, and this was witnessed by the boy, who then had to be shut up. To add spice to the story there was a further idea gaining traction that the identity of the lover in the room was in fact Samuel himself.

Any sympathy towards Samuel Kent had always been muted. He was a factory inspector who had made himself unpopular by prosecuting a local boy for stealing apples from his trees. Another local man was prosecuted for taking fish from Kent's stretch of the river. There was also the suspicion that Samuel was something of a womaniser.

Whicher believed that there was nothing particularly suspicious about the slightly contradictory testimony provided by Elizabeth Gough. He considered her to be confused and flustered rather than attempting to conceal anything. Whicher's suspicion turned to the victim's 16-year-old half-sister and, three weeks after the murder, Constance Kent was arrested.

At the committal proceedings Whicher's case looked weak. There was a missing nightdress that could not be accounted for, perhaps because it had been worn on the night of the murder and had become bloodstained, but not really much else. With little hope of a conviction, Constance was released before the case came to trial.

It looked as if the case would remain unsolved and within a few months of the murder the Kent family moved home, hoping to seek some privacy away from prying eyes. Previously the family had spent four years living in Walton-in-Gordano and they now returned to the Somerset coast to live at Camden Manor in Weston-super-Mare.

Seemingly out of the blue, five years after her stepbrother's murder Constance Kent, who had spent much of the intervening period studying in France, made a statement to a clergyman saying that she wanted to confess to the crime. Constance described how she had waited until the household was asleep, had taken the young boy from his room and slit his throat with her father's razor.

This was a controversial route to seeking justice as the clergyman now had a fine line to tread because the information had been entrusted to him in a confession. Nevertheless, as Constance was anxious to clear her conscience and see this through to the bitter end, her confession was taken to the police.

Constance Kent was tried at Salisbury Assizes on 21 July 1865, where she pleaded guilty to murder. At this point she was anxious to make it clear that she had no particular grudge towards her young victim; her real anger was directed towards her father and stepmother for the way that they spoke about her late mother, her father's first wife.

Constance Kent was convicted for the murder of her three-year-old half-brother cc

Constance was sentenced to death, but this was commuted to a life sentence owing to her having admitted to the crime and also in view of her youth at the time of the murder. She served twenty years in prison before being released at the age of 41. Within a year she had emigrated to Australia, changing her name to Ruth Emilie Kaye and training to become a nurse. She remained in Australia and lived to the age of one hundred, a stark contrast to the brief life of her stepbrother who had died so violently at the age of three.

In Kate Summerscale's excellent book on the case, *The Suspicions of Mr Whicher*, which has also been turned into a television drama, the theory is put forward that the confession was concocted in order to protect her brother William. Constance was said to be particularly close to him and shared a simmering resentment towards the seemingly preferred children of their father's second wife. Despite Constance's wish to take sole responsibility it seems quite possible that the two of them together, or possibly William alone, were the real killers of their young half-brother.

The Suspicious Case at Yeovil

SARAH PETERS HAD BEEN UNWELL FOR SOME TIME WITH A STOMACH COMPLAINT. HER CONDITION SUDDENLY DETERIORATED AND SHE DIED ON A JULY MORNING IN 1860. IN MANY PEOPLE'S MINDS THERE WAS LITTLE DOUBT THAT SHE HAD BEEN POISONED.

Silvester Peters, the husband of Sarah, had been born in 1828 at Worle, close to Weston-super-Mare, where his father had been a pig farmer. Initially Silvester found employment as a licensed hawker. Silvester and Sarah settled down in Corsham in Wiltshire and started a family before moving to Yeovil, where Silvester traded as a draper. At the time of these events Sarah was just 28 years old. The two had been married for eight years, had three children and were living above Silvester's shop in The Borough.

The diagnosis of Dr Garland, who was called in to see if he could help Sarah in her final illness, was that she was suffering from 'intense irritation of the stomach and bowels of an obscure nature'. That much would probably already have been fairly self-evident to anyone seeing Sarah in the last weeks of her life. Garland was sufficiently concerned by Sarah's condition for him to send samples off to a chemist in Bristol for a toxicology report. When the toxic element antimony was discovered, the case was referred to the Yeovil Police.

Unfortunately, before any further action could be taken, Sarah's condition took a turn for the worse. Sarah was now in more pain than ever and the doctor was urgently summoned on the evening of 4 July 1860. There was nothing that could be done and Sarah died the following morning. Under the circumstances the doctor was reticent about issuing a death certificate and a coroner's inquest was held. For its time the inquest seems to have been a particularly thorough and professionally conducted affair at which the news of the discovery of antimony was first made public. A post-mortem examination was ordered to be carried out and interestingly Silvester seemed extraordinarily reluctant to allow this. This echoed an earlier protestation that he had made to the doctor at the time of her death, when he had been adamant that the body of his wife should be left alone.

Following the post-mortem the inquest was resumed on 25 July 1860. The experts had found a number of serious internal problems within Sarah, which must have meant that she had suffered excruciating pain before dying of peritonitis. The report also added that this could have been caused by the presence of antimony and, in support of this theory, they drew the coroner's attention to the fact that the intestines were damaged and there was inflammation consistent with poisoning. In fact there were no traces of the poison in Sarah's body at the time of examination, the rationale being that since the earlier discovery of the poison any antimony could easily have passed through her body.

Throughout this period Silvester was particularly defensive. He was keen to stress that Sarah had left untouched what would have been her final meal. There seemed to be protestations of innocence at a time when he was yet to be accused of anything. If these were attempts to make sure that the finger of suspicion did not point in his direction it had exactly the opposite effect.

The jury at the inquest concluded that Sarah Peters died from 'a complication of disease accelerated by the presence of some irritant, but how and by whom administered there is no evidence before the jury to show'. This was a particularly damning verdict as it had become evident that although antimony at that time was sometimes used in medicines, no remedy administered to Sarah at that time contained antimony.

With an inconclusive verdict, Silvester Peters was free to go and he initially returned to his drapery business. Silvester and Sarah were not known to have a poor relationship and there seemed little motive for him to have murdered his wife, yet that suspicion remained in many people's minds. Whether this has any bearing on the case it is hard to know, but within a year a new woman appeared in Silvester's life, Matilda Bailey.

Silvester Peters did eventually move from Yeovil, taking Matilda with him. He surfaced again in Southampton, still plying his old trade as a draper. He stayed with

Matilda until she died in 1892 and it seems that the same year Silvester, never one to waste time in these matters, married Clara Cave, who was 26 years younger than himself. Silvester died in 1908 at the age of 80 and Clara, his third wife, was left to move in with her sister and live on in Southampton until her own death in 1928.

The Mermaid Hotel in Yeovil where the inquest into the death of Sarah Peters was held

The events surrounding the death of Sarah Peters and the inquest that followed were played out in the newspapers at the same time as the Rode murder (covered in the last chapter). While the story of the murder of Saville Kent continues to fascinate people, the suspicious death of Sarah Peters is now more or less forgotten.

The Brides in the Bath

GEORGE JOSEPH SMITH WAS A MURDERER AND BIGAMIST WITH CONNECTIONS TO BRISTOL AND WESTON-SUPER-MARE. IN 1915 HE WAS FOUND GUILTY OF MURDERING THREE WOMEN, THE CASE BECOMING WORLD-FAMOUS AS THE BRIDES IN THE BATH MURDERS.

While Smith was living in Gloucester Road in Bristol, Edith Peglar applied for a position as his housekeeper. In fact, it turned out that Edith lived with her mother just a few doors away. After knowing each other for just one week they were married at St Peter's Registry Office in Bristol on 30 July 1908.

389 Gloucester Road. The Bristol home of George Joseph Smith

© Barbara Busby

From this point onwards Smith would keep his base in Bristol. The Gloucester Road premises was set up as an antiques shop on the ground floor, which provided Smith with an excellent cover story. He could disappear for months at a time, supposedly accumulating stock from around the country and even abroad. He would often claim that his business trips were taking him to exotic places such as Spain and Canada, rather than the more prosaic truth of Herne Bay or Blackpool, where he was seeking out victims. Between 1908 and his arrest there were seven bigamous marriages. His motive, it seemed, was simply to steal each wife's savings before disappearing. Three of these marriages ended in murder.

In-between his other marriages, Smith would always come back to Edith Peglar and soon they bought another property in Southend. Links with Bristol were maintained, however, as he took out a mortgage on a further Bristol property, close to where they had the house in Gloucester Road, at Ashley Down Road. In fact, it became a regular pattern for him to invest his ill-gotten gains into property. He was to buy another six or seven houses in Bristol before he was caught.

During this time Smith seemed perfectly happy to draw attention to himself as he posed as a pillar of the community. There was a letter to the *Western Daily Press* addressed from Gloucester Road stressing the importance of parental responsibility in the raising of children, then a further opinionated letter saying that unemployment could be easily avoided if men were prepared to be more adaptable, which he finishing off by saying that 'We must adapt ourselves and always be on the move.' Smith was certainly soon on the move, as he once again travelled the country swindling women out of their money.

His first *murder* victim was Bessie Mundy. Smith, calling himself Henry Williams, married her and stole £150 in cash, before deserting her. Eighteen months later the two of them met by chance in Weston-super-Mare. Bessie was staying in a boarding house in South Road while Smith had been staying nearby in Longton Grove Road. Rather surprisingly Bessie almost instantly forgave Smith for his behaviour.

Wanting to make things right between them, Smith took Bessie to a solicitor in Waterloo Street to set up a repayment plan for the money that he had previously tricked her out of. In reality Smith had his eye on a further £2,500 which he knew she had. On Smith's suggestion, they drew up mutual wills, whereby each would benefit in the event of the other's death. Less than a week later Bessie would be dead, having drowned in her bath in Herne Bay, supposedly following a fit.

In November 1913, Smith married Alice Burnham. He had hit on a method that worked well for him. Soon after the marriage he persuaded her to make a will. The newlyweds went to Blackpool on their honeymoon and, after Alice was found dead in the bath, Smith inherited £600.

Posing as an estate agent called John Lloyd, Smith married his third victim, Margaret Lofty. She was to drown in their lodgings in London. With this latest case being reported in the national newspapers, and each death having being so similar, at last people

George Joseph Smith, The Brides in the Bath murderer cc

were starting to notice a pattern. The landlord from a Blackpool boarding house spotted the similarities and alerted the London Police.

On 1 February 1915, Smith was arrested just as he was leaving a solicitor's office having sorted out his latest wife's will. With Smith arrested for the charge of bigamy and on suspicion of murder, the pathologist Bernard Spilsbury was asked to determine how the women had died. An immediate problem was that, looking at the bathtubs in question, they all seemed a little on the small side for someone to accidentally drown. Spilsbury reasoned that Smith must have seized his victims by the feet and suddenly pulled them up towards himself, sliding the upper part of their body underwater. The sudden flood of water into the victim's nose and throat might cause shock and sudden loss of consciousness, explaining the absence of injuries and minimal signs of drowning.

George Joseph Smith was formally charged with the murders of Bessie, Alice and Margaret on 23 March 1915. Three months later, on 22 June, the trial began at the Old Bailey and the full picture of Smith began to emerge. He had been born in East London. From a very early age he was in trouble for swindling and theft. In 1896, he was imprisoned for twelve months for persuading a woman to steal from her employers. There had been elaborate police investigations in over 40 towns in England and there were over 150 statements from witnesses, 100 of whom were to testify at Smith's trial.

Smith was held at Maidstone Prison awaiting his execution, scheduled for 13 August 1915. He filled his time sending letters in which he was anxious to stress that he was innocent of all the charges.

The Porlock Tragedy

HENRY QUARTLY HAD ENJOYED A PERFECTLY CORDIAL RELATIONSHIP WITH HIS NEIGHBOURS IN PORLOCK, BUT THEN THINGS SUDDENLY DETERIORATED. IN DECEMBER 1913 QUARTLY WAS PUT BEFORE THE DUNSTER MAGISTRATES FOR HAVING USED INDECENT LANGUAGE WITHIN HEARING OF THE HIGHWAY. THINGS ESCALATED AND IN MAY 1914 HE WAS AGAIN SUMMONED FOR BEHAVING IN AN INSULTING MANNER TOWARDS HIS NEIGHBOURS. THIS TIME QUARTLY TOOK MATTERS INTO HIS OWN HANDS.

Henry's father had been a stonemason and he and his brother both followed him into the same trade. After his father's death Henry lived on in the family home with his sister Emily in Parson's Street, Porlock.

The neighbours with whom Quartly argued so disastrously were Henry and Fanny Pugsley. It had been Fanny who had been the main complainant regarding Quartly's language. Mr Pugsley was 59 years of age, four years older than Quartly, and had spent some time working as a servant on a nearby farm in Porlock. By 1911 he was a fish merchant and fruiterer and living with Fanny and their stepson, William. Fanny was also local to the area, having been born about eight miles from Porlock.

On Wednesday 3 June 1914, Quartly's neighbours came home and Pugsley stabled their horse before walking up the path to his house. Quartly was in his own garden at the time and two ladies, Alice Middleton and a Mrs Chapman, were chatting nearby. They witnessed Quartly produce a shotgun and, from a distance of about twenty feet, casually shoot Pugsley. The wounded man was hit in the back, close to the right shoulder.

While Fanny rushed to help her dying husband a policeman who had fortuitously been close at hand, Constable Greedy, quickly assessed the situation. Greedy chased Quartly back into the house where it seemed he now hoped to end his own life. However, his second shot, intended for himself, only grazed his face and before he could reload the policeman was able to take the gun from him and make an arrest. Quartly didn't appear to have done himself much damage with the suicide attempt (other than blow off half of his moustache) and he was marched off to Dunster police station.

Quartly was searched and a note was found in his pocket which read, 'I got no grievance against anyone else only those two Pugsleys. They are the most dangerous crew I

The old Dunster police station where Quartly was taken on arrest

ever knew and have only got to thank themselves, they started it.'

Quartly was tried at Taunton on 20 October 1914. It was all over fairly swiftly, as Quartly would have nothing to do with his own counsel for the defence. The judge tried to persuade him otherwise as, despite the fact that the accused was anxious to assert his guilt, there might be other circumstances that needed to be considered. The defendant just wanted it over with and to get on with reading his goodbye speech.

Quartly seems to have been a very popular local character and, while it is hard to see how the Pugsleys could have inspired such hatred in him, it is difficult not to be impressed with his panache at his trial, which, as a result of his guilty plea, lasted barely twelve minutes. He interrupted the judge's summing-up to make sure that it was on record that he had wished that he had shot Pugsley's wife as well. Then, with the sentence of death passed, he announced to those in the crowded courtroom that he was sorry to be leaving his old friends behind but that he hoped that they would keep their peckers up and that he hoped to meet them all again some day. As he left the courtroom he cheerfully shouted, 'Goodbye all!' Quartly was hanged at Shepton Mallet Prison on Tuesday 10 November 1914.

The Frome Murder

ON 24 SEPTEMBER 1851 SARAH WATTS WAS LOOKING AFTER
BATTLE FARM, WHERE SHE LIVED, WHILE HER PARENTS
WERE AWAY AT THE MARKET. THEY RETURNED AT ABOUT
FOUR O'CLOCK THAT AFTERNOON BUT INITIALLY COULD FIND
NO SIGN OF THEIR FOURTEEN-YEAR-OLD DAUGHTER. THERE
WAS, HOWEVER, SOME BLOOD ON THE FLOOR AND THEIR
INVESTIGATIONS QUICKLY TOOK THEM TO THE DAIRY, WHERE
SARAH'S BATTERED BODY WAS DISCOVERED.

It was later found that there were some trivial items
missing from the house and the initial belief was that
perhaps Sarah had surprised a burglar. Something else
out of the ordinary was that the intruder seemed to have
rather clumsily left a silk handkerchief on the table.

Suspicion quickly fell on three local men: Robert Hurd,
William Sparrow and William Maggs. People reported
that they had been heard around noon making an
arrangement to meet up. By two o'clock they were
spotted in the region of the farm, which was about two
miles from Frome. As the police enquiries progressed
they began to build up a pretty comprehensive picture
of the gang's movements. By 3pm they were spotted
again in the region of the house and later still they were

seen again, but this time they had suspiciously changed into different clothing.

All of the sightings of the gang were purely circumstantial evidence until one witness was able to say that they had actually seen Maggs passing something to Hurd, and that he had also been overheard talking about a watch. As a watch was among the items stolen from the Watts' farm, this seemed to be particularly damning evidence. While Maggs and Hurd were incriminated by the watch, William Sparrow was in even deeper trouble when someone was able to state that the handkerchief found at the scene of the crime belonged to him.

In fact Sparrow had already been particularly indiscreet as he had mentioned that he had seen the body in the dairy. This was an extraordinary admission as this would have to have been before the police arrived. His understanding was that Sarah had been beaten with a stick, and he said that he knew exactly who was responsible.

With some justification Maggs now believed that Sparrow was totally incapable of keeping his mouth shut. But it was now his turn to be overheard. As far as this latest eavesdropper could ascertain, the murder was a bungled robbery that had been organised by Hurd. Maggs supposedly said that he believed that Sparrow would be lured into giving evidence against his accomplices by the substantial reward that was now on offer.

The inquest was held at the George Inn, West Woodlands and it was now revealed that Sarah's death was in fact caused by strangulation. The police tried to build up a picture of the day of the murder. Several witnesses, who were largely drawn from the pubs frequented by the accused, were able to add to the already pretty comprehensive list of the suspects' movements. The newspapers referred to them as 'desperados' and there certainly seems to have been no shortage of people coming forward and enthusiastically giving evidence in the hope of perhaps seeing the last of the gang.

Despite Hurd, Maggs and Sparrow being arrested within six days of the murder, it took six months for the case to come to court. The three men were tried at the Taunton Assizes on 6 April 1852 where, despite the wealth of circumstantial evidence, the case still fell apart.

A likely scenario seemed to be that Hurd had planned the robbery but there was every possibility that he had not been there when Sparrow and Maggs carried out the crime. The most likely murderer seemed to be Sparrow. Although Sparrow claimed that the incriminating handkerchief was simply not his, there was still the evidence of him talking about having seen the body of Sarah shortly after the murder. There was also a mysterious bite-mark on his hand. His explanation for the injury was that he had damaged his hand while fighting at the fair. Meanwhile the watch, initially thought to have been stolen, was in fact found to have been purchased quite legitimately. The three men were found not guilty.

The desperados were not to stay out of trouble for long, however. William Maggs had burglary charges lodged against him within months of his acquittal. This was in connection with a separate case and this time he was found guilty and sentenced to deportation. In 1853 he was in the newspapers again in connection with a daring escape from Wilton Gaol in Taunton, firstly from his cell and then over the walls by means of a concealed rope. He lasted just a few hours on the run before being recaptured.

Robert Hurd seemed to stay out of trouble, albeit that he married into the Maggs family, but 'The Notorious Bill Sparrow', as he came to be known (most felt that he had escaped pretty lightly at the trial for Sarah's murder) was soon in trouble again. Like Maggs, Sparrow was convicted of burglary and, also like Maggs, he managed to escape from prison, although this time it was Wells Gaol where he was being held. He and another prisoner, still in their chains, burrowed their way out. They managed to evade capture until the next day when they were caught hiding in a field conveniently close to Shepton Mallet Prison.

In the meantime no further arrests were made in connection with Sarah's murder. In 1861 a local man confessed, but this confession turned out to be a total fabrication as the suspect was not even in the country at the time. None of the three men tried for murder ever admitted to any involvement in Sarah's death and so it seems we will never know exactly what happened at Battle Farm.

Partial remains of Taunton Gaol from where Maggs escaped

The Hunt for the Bristol Wife Murderer

IN MARCH 1904 THERE WAS GREAT EXCITEMENT AT THE NEWS OF THE CAPTURE OF A MAN, ARRESTED IN SALFORD, FOR PASSING A FORGED BANK NOTE. THE PRISONER CLAIMED TO BE BRISTOL'S MOST WANTED MAN AND EVERYONE WAS NOW CONFIDENT THAT AT LAST THE FIVE-YEAR SEARCH FOR THE NOTORIOUS

Contemporary drawing of Hayball circulated at the time of his disappearance

MURDERER FREDERICK WILLIAM HAYBALL WAS FINALLY OVER.

Frederick Hayball had married Ellen Milson on 5 April 1886. She was just eighteen while her husband was five years older. By the time of Hayball's disappearance they had been married for thirteen unhappy years. Frederick was a sailor and during his brief time at home there was a shocking list of violence against Ellen. In fact, soon after their wedding Fred had received a sentence of two weeks in gaol for violence against his wife. Fortunately, Frederick was away a fair amount in those early years, during which time Ellen was living in Hereford Street in Bedminster with her mother, Ann Milson who, like Ellen, worked as a tailoress.

By 1898 Hayball had more or less given up his life at sea and was making a living as a longshoreman working in the docks. Now that he was at home more than he had ever been before throughout the marriage, the violence started to escalate. After serving his latest sentence for violent behaviour, Hayball went home and once more attacked Ellen, at the same time telling her if she had him arrested again he would kill her. Despite the warning, the next time he was violent towards her she sent for the police. When Hayball was released in May 1899, he killed Ellen with a hatchet.

It was a neighbour, Laura Gilks, who discovered Ellen's body at the house, which was in a small courtyard off Avon Street. She went to find a policeman and while PC White was at the house examining the body and looking for evidence, Laura headed for the local pub, the Cross Guns, in nearby Temple Street. As it was the May Bank Holiday she knew Hayball would not be at work and would very likely be enjoying a drink. Indeed Hayball was in the bar and when Laura confronted him it seems that he did at least consider the possibility of handing himself in. He said that he would have one last drink and then return home to face the music. Within five minutes of the conversation with Laura the police were at the Cross Guns, but Hayball was gone.

A description of the fugitive was circulated. Hayball was five feet nine in height, with dark brown hair and brown eyes. At the time of his disappearance he had been wearing a dark coat with a patch on one shoulder, moleskin trousers and a cap. It was thought that he may have escaped from the area on a goods train. As a child Hayball had lived in Sussex Street, close to the old St Philips railway station and, despite his time away at sea, he would have known the streets well.

With no immediate success in locating him, word was spread to ports overseas. San Francisco was seen as a particularly probable destination. It was a route that would be known to Hayball as he had made at least two voyages from Bristol to San Francisco via Australia. Attention was diverted to the ships that left England and Wales, on that route, between 20 and 31 May 1899. Of the six likely ships, two were from London, the remainder from either Swansea or Cardiff.

Fully briefed on the Hayball case, the San Francisco Police were confident of getting their man. Recently they had enjoyed great success in capturing a fugitive called Frank Butler, who was wanted for the murder

Bedminster Police Station, where the inquest into the death of Ellen Hayball was held cc

of several gold prospectors and was arrested on a ship called the *Swanhilda* as it arrived from Australia into San Francisco harbour. Flushed with this success it seemed that the arrest of Hayball would be little more than a formality. But as each ship arrived there was no sign of the wanted man.

Back in Bristol there was talk of his body being fished out of the docks, Hayball having killed himself, but this proved to be untrue. Likewise, on 29 August the London Police incorrectly announced that he had been apprehended in Canada. Some newspapers became

37

convinced he was hiding in Edinburgh but this, like all the other leads, came to nothing.

Five years later, the news came from Salford that Hayball had been taken into custody. Police from Bristol were despatched to collect the fugitive, who claimed that he had been residing in America until the last few weeks. Once again all the optimism was misplaced, as the man turned out to be a criminal recently released from prison, known as John Morgan, who had spent the previous five years in gaol. His latest activities involving the forged money earned him a further six months in prison.

There were to be no further sightings. Hayball had well and truly disappeared.

The Dundry Murder

GEORGE AND SARAH WATERMAN LIVED IN A SECLUDED SPOT IN DUNDRY, NORTH SOMERSET. IN THE EARLY EVENING OF 9 JANUARY 1861 THEY WERE TRICKED INTO OPENING THEIR FRONT DOOR TO TWO STRANGERS. THE ELDERLY COUPLE WERE THEN SUBJECTED TO A VIOLENT ROBBERY IN THE COURSE OF WHICH SARAH WAS MURDERED.

Normally George would have been more careful about opening the door but when one of his unexpected visitors claimed to be 'John, the Winsford policeman' he was reassured. He was then struck on the head with a wooden club by one of the two intruders, who demanded to know where he kept his money. Sarah, who had been sewing beside the fire, was given similar treatment. George was then locked in the pantry while the intruders made off with a few shillings, a couple of watches, various keepsakes and George's service medals. The haul from the robbery was a great deal less than what the robbers had been expecting to find there.

With the attackers now gone, George was able to escape from his captivity and get help from a neighbour. Doctor Shorland was summoned but by now an hour had passed since the attack and Sarah's condition was deteriorating. Within a further half an hour she was dead from the four blows received to her head. Fortunately for him, George's injuries proved to be less serious.

The inquest into Sarah's death was held at the Dundry Inn, which was about 250 yards from the scene of the attack. The first people in the frame for the robbery and murder were actually George's own nephews, although until recently neither of them had been known to the Watermans. They were Matthew and Charles Wedmore, who had been brought up in the Bedminster area of Bristol. Matthew, the older of the two, was now 32 years of age and worked in the Bristol docks. Charles was just 24, and a private in the Marine Artillery.

It emerged that just prior to the attack Charles Wedmore had visited the Watermans. Unsure of the exact address, a local man named John Keevil had kindly shown him the property. Keevil had once served as the village policeman but was now a gardener. As he arrived at the Watermans' house he had declared his identity from the other side of the door so that Sarah would open up. It seemed that Wedmore had remembered the words to use should he need to gain access to the house at a later date.

On the night of the murder Charles and Matthew had been seen drinking in the village. Perhaps they were getting the Dutch courage they were going to need for the night's work. George's watches soon surfaced when they were offered to Jeremiah Jordan, the landlord of a beer house called the Thetis Frigate in Bristol. Jones was able to identify the Wedmores as the ones trying to sell these stolen items.

The brothers were arrested in Hotwell Road in Bristol. Both prisoners put up a desperate fight, and Matthew fired off a loaded pistol at one of the constables when within about three yards of him. Despite the fact that they were armed (Charles was also carrying a pistol which he attempted to fire) they were successfully apprehended and taken to Clifton police station. George was able to recognise them as being the murderers. He also recognised the guns that they had used so ineffectively at the time of the arrest as being his own property, stolen in the robbery. Realising that things were looking a bit bleak for them, the first thing the brothers did was to issue statements blaming each other.

The trial started in Taunton in March 1861. The immediate trigger for the attack soon became apparent. The brothers were aware of a recent house sale by George and they could reasonably have expected to find the proceeds concealed in the house. In fact they were right: the money was there, they had just failed to find it.

From the moment they were found guilty of Sarah's murder, the brothers did not see each other again until the morning of their execution, when they met in the gaol chapel. They were hanged together in Taunton, watched by a crowd of 7,000 people.

William Calcraft, who executed the Wedmore brothers at Taunton Gaol on 5 April 1861

George Waterman, who had survived the attack, slowly recovered from his injuries. A few months after the execution of his assailants, he is recorded as living with his nephew, Thomas, in Wells. Soon afterwards he went to live in Crediton in Devon where he lived for the next sixteen years before dying at the age of 91.

The Baby Murders

AMELIA DYER WAS EXECUTED ON 10 JUNE 1896. SHE WAS ONE OF THE MOST PROLIFIC SERIAL KILLERS IN HISTORY AND ALTHOUGH THE STORY ENDS ON THE SCAFFOLD OF NEWGATE PRISON IT ALL BEGAN IN BRISTOL BACK IN 1837.

Amelia Dyer at the time of her final arrest cc

Amelia Elizabeth Hobley was born in a small village just to the east of Bristol. She was the daughter of a master shoemaker, Samuel Hobley. Her mother, Sarah was never well throughout her daughter's childhood and died when Amelia was eleven years of age. After her mother's death Amelia stayed on in Bristol, living with one of her aunts. By 1861 she was married to George Thomas, who was more than thirty years older than herself.

Amelia commenced training to become a nurse and as a result she could not have failed to come into contact with the practice of baby farming. This involved individuals supposedly acting as adoption agents, in return for a payment. There was usually a one-off fee to take an unwanted or unaffordable child away. Once the mother was off the scene the child was often neglected.

Before long Amelia began advertising her services, offering a loving home for unwanted children. Some certainly died of natural causes, but she clearly saw the need to increase turnover and at some point took to murdering the babies more or less as soon as they were placed in her care.

It seems incredible that it took so long for Amelia to come to the attention of the police. In 1879 a doctor did point out that there seemed to be rather a lot of child deaths involving Amelia and as a result she was sentenced to six months' hard labour for neglect.

In the 1880s Amelia was living in the St Paul's area of Bristol and calling herself a laundress. By now her first husband was dead and Amelia had married William Dyer, who was six years younger than herself and worked in a Bristol brewery. They had two children together before they eventually split up. William seemed to struggle to be rid of Amelia and as late as August 1894, by which time he had left the family home and was living in the Stapleton area of Bristol, he was still placing public notices in the local Bristol paper stating that he would not be held accountable for any of his wife's debts. Although William had started to call himself a widower, this was far from the case, as Amelia was very much alive and building up to the most prolific killing spree of her life.

There is little doubt that Amelia had spells in mental hospitals due to her instability. There were several attempts at suicide. At one point she drank two whole bottles of laudanum. There was also an attempt to drown herself in Bristol on 26 April 1894 when she was dragged out of a stream in Ashton Park to the west of the city. She was taken by the police to the General Hospital on Guinea Street suffering from the effects of immersion in water. Had she not survived that suicide attempt there is no doubt that a great many lives would have been saved.

After her spell in gaol Amelia returned to her life of crime, but she now resolved to be more careful and where possible to avoid the involvement of either doctors or death certificates. After a while she moved away from Bristol and started to use various aliases, making it difficult to track her movements. Certainly by 1895 she had moved to Caversham and then to nearby Reading.

In January 1896, there began a sequence of events that led to Amelia finally being apprehended. Evelina Marmon, a barmaid from Cheltenham, gave birth to an illegitimate daughter. After she read an advertisement in the newspaper from a Mrs Harding, who seemed anxious to adopt a young child, a meeting was arranged. A fee was paid to Amelia (of course it was her once again, using an alias) and she was entrusted with the baby.

Soon after, the bodies of two strangled babies, one of which was Evelina's child, were carefully packed into a bag, along with bricks for added weight, and dropped into the weir at Caversham Lock. This was a location that Amelia had used before and as a result it was one that was already under surveillance. A bargeman had seen a brown paper parcel half submerged near the bank, in which there was found the body of a baby. The packaging had links to Amelia, including a label from Bristol Temple Meads and even a faint name and address.

The following morning police raided Amelia's home. While there were no babies to be found, there was a wealth of incriminating evidence in the form of paraphernalia and letters associated with babies that she was supposed to have adopted. Amelia Dyer was arrested and charged with murder.

On 22 May 1896, Dyer appeared at the Old Bailey and pleaded guilty to the murder of Doris Marmon, the daughter of the Cheltenham barmaid. The defence offered by Dyer was one of insanity, and it was undeniably true that she had spent periods in asylums in Bristol and Gloucester. Nevertheless, it took the jury only four and a half minutes to find her guilty of murder.

It is uncertain how many more children Amelia Dyer may have killed. At the time of her death it seemed she was responsible for just a handful of murders. The Thames in the region of Caversham Lock was dredged and six more bodies were discovered, but there can be little doubt she was responsible for many more. Some estimates put the figure at a staggeringly high figure of several hundred, but it is hard to be precise.

There were reports of Amelia's unnerving behaviour while she awaited her execution in gaol. She was said to just stare, unblinking, at the guards in her cell for hours on end. There was also supposed to be a letter that she sent to her daughter in which she said that she had no soul: it had been 'hammered out of her while in Gloucester Asylum'.

Murder of a Policeman near Yeovil

NATHANIEL COX WAS THE VILLAGE POLICEMAN FOR EAST COKER IN SOMERSET, WHERE HE LIVED WITH HIS WIFE, MARY ANN AND HIS CHILDREN. ON 16 NOVEMBER 1876 HE WAS ON DUTY WITH A FELLOW POLICEMAN, HENRY STACEY, WHEN THEY WERE ATTACKED. STACEY WAS KNOCKED UNCONSCIOUS BUT SURVIVED, WHILE COX WAS KILLED.

The two policemen had been detailed to keep their eyes peeled for any petty crimes that might occur at the Yeovil fair. The first significant event of that fateful evening was when they were at Netherton, about three miles from Yeovil, and they noted a horse and cart approaching them along a narrow lane. The cart appeared to be empty and was accompanied by three, or possibly four, men. It was the same cart that they encountered a couple of hours later in an almost identical place. The cart now looked as if it might be loaded and while one man drove, the other three walked at the side. Cox stopped the cart in order to question the men while Stacey attempted to see what exactly was being conveyed. Before Cox's interview of the men could get under way he was knocked to the ground by a brutal blow to the head.

Realising that Cox was now in trouble, Stacey ran to give assistance but likewise he was attacked and knocked out cold. Stacey struggled back to consciousness and despite collapsing several times was eventually able to make his way to a nearby farm.

The farmer and a couple of his labourers now returned to the scene of the crime. The cart was long gone, but they found Nathaniel Cox by the side of the road. They took the body to the pub in East Coker and the doctor was summoned. Cox was now attended by Dr Garland, the same doctor whose vigilance, some years earlier, had cast doubt over the death of Sarah Peters described earlier in this book. There was nothing that could be done for Cox but Stacey was taken to hospital, where he remained in a critical condition for several weeks.

A police notice was circulated and one of the wanted men, Charles Baker, a 36-year-old labourer, was soon arrested. While his hiding place (his own house) may have lacked sophistication, the others involved remained elusive. The three other men thought to have carried out the attack were known poachers: George Hutchings and his two sons, Giles and Peter. The exact ages vary between accounts and, to add to that confusion, Peter was really called George Jnr, but a different name was used in order to avoid confusion between them.

At one time the Hutchings family were living at 81 Back Street in the middle of Yeovil and subsequently in Hardington Road. George classed himself as a general labourer while Mary, George's wife and mother to Peter and Giles, called herself a glover (Yeovil was a major centre for glove-making). Giles had also at one time attempted to become a glover before embarking on a life of petty crime.

There were to be several sightings of the fugitives but they managed to stay one step in front of the law until a surprising new development occurred. James Vagg, a butcher from West Coker, arrived at Yeovil police station with old George Hutchings and Giles in his cart. Both were dishevelled and dirty. He claimed to have found them by the side of the road near East Chinnock. This was 20 January, two months after the murder and, having endured a harsh winter on the run, they were now happy to give themselves up.

Peter did not last long on the run by himself. Within two days he was discovered in a hayloft, arrested and charged with murder along with the others. All four men eventually appeared at Taunton Assizes charged with the murder of PC Cox and the attempted murder of PC Stacey. One of the main conundrums faced by the

The Shire Hall in Taunton. The jury took under an hour to bring back a verdict of manslaughter

jury was the fact that it was unlikely that all four men were equally culpable for delivering the fatal blow. There was a problem in apportioning the guilt.

The theory of the prosecution was that the four men had intended to go poaching but did not fancy it once it had come on to rain. But if the poaching expedition had been abandoned and the cart was empty, then why did violence instantly erupt when the policeman wanted to look in the cart? Clearly the cart was not empty the second time that it was encountered and so it must have contained incriminating evidence.

In addition to this there was also the fact that the family seemed to have a particular grudge against the police force which, they felt, was continually harassing them.

Looking at the old police records it becomes clear that although Baker and George seemed to be reasonably law-abiding, that was not the case with George's two sons, who appear to have carried on a running battle with the police. Giles had just been released from a six-month sentence, served in Taunton, for assaulting a police officer, and back in 1872 Peter and Giles had both received a sentence of one month's hard labour for a previous assault on another policeman.

This time the judge handed each of them a sentence of 24 years' imprisonment. Baker asked permission to speak and informed the judge that the old man had had nothing to do with the affray, but had driven the cart on and did not know what had taken place. Sure enough, while the other three were moved on from Taunton Gaol to Millbank Prison a message arrived from the Home Secretary which granted a free pardon to George Hutchings Senior.

Riddle of a Bruise

REGINALD IVOR HINKS HAD ALWAYS HOPED TO RUN HIS OWN BUSINESS. HE HAD PLANS TO SET UP A CLEANING SERVICE AND TESTED THE MARKET BY BECOMING A VACUUM CLEANER SALESMAN IN BATH. HE MET CONSTANCE, HIS FUTURE WIFE, WHILE OUT TRYING TO SELL HIS PRODUCTS. SHE WAS ATTRACTED BY HIS CHARM AND GOOD LOOKS; HE WAS ATTRACTED BY HER FATHER'S MONEY.

Constance's father, James Pullen, had worked for most of his life as a tailor. When Connie was young the family lived at 18 Hart Road in Dorking. They then lived for some time in Westbury, where Constance met and married her first husband.

At the time that Constance met and swiftly married Reginald Hinks in 1933, she was divorced and was living in Milton Avenue in Bath. Her father was now in his eighties and had become confused with age and, although Constance looked after him, she also had a nurse to assist her. They lived quite comfortably and still maintained a small portfolio of properties in Bath and Dorking.

Hinks was 32 years old and in his youth had been an apprentice at the famous old engineering works of Stothert and Pitt in Bath. But before long he had traded

Reginald Ivor Hinks. Although born in South Africa, he had lived in Bath since he had been a young boy

Bill Walden

in his lodgings in Twerton for the bright lights of London, working as a barman in Lambeth and then a cloakroom attendant in a London club.

Very soon after meeting and marrying Connie, Hinks moved into their house in Poets' Corner. The nurse was dismissed and Hinks personally started to care for the befuddled old man. Soon the three of them moved up the road to a more impressive house in Englishcombe Lane.

Losing patience at his father-in-law's longevity, and anxious to get his hands on more of the money, Hinks now attempted to help poor old James on his way. The first attempts involved leaving the old man to fend for himself in the centre of town in the hope that he would get himself run over. When James survived this he attempted to drown him in the bath at home. Confident that this scheme had worked, he called the police only to find that by the time they arrived his father-in-law had recovered. The attempted drowning was on 30 November 1933 and it seems that Hinks could not wait even a full 24 hours before having another go at polishing the old man off. This time he was successful. James Pullen was gassed to death in what Hinks was hoping would be seen as suicide.

At the inquest, however, the finger of suspicion seemed to be slowly pointing towards Hinks. He had explained to the police, at the scene of the crime, how Pullen's head had hit the floor as he pulled him away from the oven and it was this that had caused bruising. This may have been a plausible explanation for the bruise on the back of Pullen's head, but the fact was that at this point the bruise had not even been noticed. To some it looked like a slightly over-eager attempt to establish his innocence.

The nurse, who had been promptly dismissed by Hinks when he took over caring for Pullen, now gave evidence. She spoke of how Pullen was desperately unhappy about his diminished state and of the suicide threats that he had made. Suddenly Hinks's account of events seemed rather more probable. However, she also confirmed that Pullen would have had no understanding of how the gas in the kitchen worked. Also, there had clearly been a fair amount of preparatory work involved, such as the removal of the oven shelves and sealing the room up, which she felt Pullen was no longer capable of planning. At the end of the inquest the jury took less than half an hour to return their verdict of wilful murder against Hinks.

The five-day trial commenced at the Old Bailey on 5 March 1934. In addition to the evidence previously presented there was further medical testimony which seemed to support Hinks. It suggested that the contentious bruise on the back of the victim's head could only have come from his being pulled away from the gas oven by his ankles. If this had been accepted as fact, Hinks would most likely have been exonerated. However, other experts disputed this evidence and said that it was far more likely that the bruise had resulted from a simple bang on the head, the implication being that the blow had been delivered by Hinks prior to putting Pullen's head in the oven. The jury took an hour and three quarters to return a guilty verdict.

Hinks had been cross-examined for well over three hours and had made a good impression with his dignified behaviour in the dock. Despite this, he continued to be depicted as a seemingly irresistible deceiver of women. The newspapers reported how the three women jurors were overcome with emotion when he was found guilty; one of them was near to collapse and needed smelling salts. The Sunday papers ran stories full of supposed revelations from women who had fallen victim to 'this unscrupulous Don Juan'. The facts, however, were that there had been comparatively few other women in his life and nothing that seemed illegal in his dealings with them. In the cold light of day he was being found guilty for a crime for which there was really only circumstantial evidence. Hinks was executed at Bristol Prison on 3 May 1934.

A Bristol Tragedy

ADA JAMES WAS THE DAUGHTER OF A BRISTOL BOOTMAKER. IN 1913 SHE WAS 22 YEARS OLD AND WORKING IN THE NAIL AND BUTTON FACTORY IN ST JAMES'S SQUARE. ADA WAS ALSO ENGAGED TO BE MARRIED TO THE MAN WHO WOULD EVENTUALLY BE EXECUTED FOR HER MURDER.

Ada's boyfriend was Ted Palmer. They had become engaged at Christmas and hoped to marry around the forthcoming Easter. Ted lived slightly to the north of Ada in Albany Place, Montpelier with his mother. He had been brought up in Bean Street in St Philip's and had lived at a series of addresses in this area.

Ted Palmer had a police record, but only for petty crimes. In 1908 he had been in court for the crime of stealing apples and then two years later for stealing cucumbers. By 1913 he had moved on from greengrocery and was enjoying a fairly chequered career. For some time he had been a boxer, then a chairmaker and the previous year he had spent largely in Canada. He was now back home, unemployed and said to be behaving strangely.

On 27 January 1913, with her after-work bible class completed, Ada returned to her house at 3 Clark's Buildings at about 7.30pm and found Ted waiting. He wanted a chat and a walk and the two of them headed off to the nearby hill at Narroways. Although they were undoubtedly on good terms to start with, something clearly went wrong, and it may be that Ted's subsequent account of what passed between them is accurate. He claimed that he had started to outline his latest scheme of a trip to the Caribbean, where he would quickly make his fortune and send for Ada. This new scheme didn't quite get the reception that he had been hoping for as Ada promptly called off the engagement. Ted claimed not to remember much else.

Ada was found in Mina Road, mortally wounded, with a cut to the throat. The quick thinking of an off-duty constable resulted in some crucial evidence. The officer was one of the first on the scene and, seeing that Ada was unable to speak, passed her an old envelope to write on. Palmer was named as her killer. Ada was then taken to the Royal Infirmary where she died of her wound.

Ted's attempt at escape was a pretty confusing affair. His first stop was to purchase pen and paper, presumably to write some sort of confession. He tried two shops in the hope of finding some stationery before heading off to Hodders the chemists to get some laudanum. He was able to acquire the drug on the basis that he was treating his toothache.

Soon Palmer was back at his grandmother's house, where he planned to have a wash and swallow the poison in the hope of ending it all. Having survived the suicide bid without the slightest ill-effects he then left the house for a further aimless wander around the familiar streets, visiting some of his old haunts for what was likely to be the last time. He was arrested, still walking the streets, at two o'clock the following morning.

Ted Palmer's trial started on 19 February 1913. He seemed in remarkably high spirits as he entered the court to plead not guilty. This strange optimism soon proved to be misplaced. Ted was revealed to have been carrying a razor in his pocket on the fateful evening. It was an action which seemed to suggest an element of premeditation. When pressed about the razor, Palmer's family explained that he had needed to buy this new one following the confiscation of his original razor, which he had been using to threaten people. The explanation did little to impress the jury who took 15 minutes to find Palmer guilty. Edward Palmer was executed on 19 March 1913.

The Shaftesbury Crusade Institute, where Ada James spent the last evening of her life, as it is today

The Leigh Woods Murder

ON 11 SEPTEMBER 1857 A MEMBER OF STAFF FROM LEIGH COURT, A STATELY HOME SITUATED TO THE NORTH-WEST OF BRISTOL, DISCOVERED A POOL OF BLOOD WHICH HAD BEEN PARTIALLY CONCEALED BY UNDERGROWTH. LEADING AWAY FROM THE BLOOD THERE WERE FOOTPRINTS HEADING

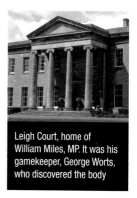

Leigh Court, home of William Miles, MP. It was his gamekeeper, George Worts, who discovered the body

TOWARDS THE NEARBY CLIFF EDGE. HE MADE HIS WAY TO THE PRECIPICE AND, LOOKING DOWN TO THE ROCKS BELOW, COULD MAKE OUT THE SHAPE OF A BODY.

The corpse was found to be that of a woman, young and dressed in a grey dress. Her injuries included a bullet wound to the head and a cut throat. Identification initially proved to be tricky. The pocket of her dress had been removed and the only immediate clue to her identity was a handkerchief which was found nearby and bore the initials C.P.

Most of the clues to who the woman might be came from the clothing itself. By working out where the clothes had been purchased or mended they were able to come to the conclusion that it was Charlotte Pugsley. Charlotte was a woman in her early thirties, although she looked younger, who had spent her formative years living in Taunton. She had also lived for some time in Bristol, as a servant to a tallow chandler (candle maker), and had recently been working in Freshford as a servant to a Mr Bythesea, who reported that Charlotte had left his employment a few days earlier and was, he understood, now with a friend of hers called John William Beale. As far as he was aware the two of them had met some years before when they were both in the service of the Hutchinson family in Clifton.

Although Beale was a native of Somerset (he was the son of a shopkeeper in Bath) he was known to have been working a hundred miles away as a butler in Northamptonshire. He was employed by a Captain Watkins, who himself was an interesting character, although he died within six months of these events after a tragic accident on the railway.

A few days before the murder Beale had been granted compassionate leave by Watkins following the news that his father had supposedly been injured and his sister had dropped down dead on hearing the news. Beale's sojourn back in Bristol was to last about a week. He was spotted a couple of times by old acquaintances and when explaining his movements to them he said that he was on his way to Bath. In fact it was at this time that he met up with Charlotte. They left her suitcases at the left luggage in Limpley Stoke station and set off to Bristol together.

With Beale as the prime suspect, the police simply needed to wait for him to return to Northamptonshire. When he did turn up at his employer he had plenty of incriminating evidence. This included two guns, one of which had been recently fired, and a bloodstained knife. By now he had clearly had a chance to collect the suitcases from the station as he also seemed to have most of Charlotte's belongings.

Beale had been caught out by the speed with which the police had managed to locate him. His first statements were rambling and full of contradictions; nevertheless, they seemed to suggest that Charlotte was no more than a friend and that he had been anxious to help her have a fresh start with her new fiancé. He explained that he had simply been accompanying Charlotte to meet her intended in Bristol. When she had safely been united with this new boyfriend of hers he had set off home to Daventry.

An initial enquiry into the case brought forward no suspects other than Beale. It also saw various witnesses placing both Charlotte and Beale walking together towards Leigh Woods. Crucially, there was also a later sighting of Beale – this time by himself – heading in the opposite direction.

A fellow employee of Charlotte's at Leigh Court had been taken into her confidence. Apparently Charlotte had spoken of a fiancé, but the man that she was talking about was quite definitely Beale. She also told her friend of a forthcoming marriage in Southampton before setting off to start a new life on the other side of the Atlantic. She said that all that stood in their way was the necessity for Beale to complete a couple of quick chores in Bristol.

The trial of Beale took place in Bourton in December 1857. With his guilt swiftly established, there was at least some sort of confession from the condemned man, albeit one that was not entirely believable. Beale claimed that when Charlotte started to pressurise him into marriage (and by now it had emerged that Beale was in fact already married) he panicked and shot her. But there was no convincing explanation as to why he was heavily armed as he went for a stroll in the woods. The explanation for cutting her throat was that she was groaning too much and he didn't want her to give the game away. She was thrown over the side of the Avon Gorge in attempt to hide the body. It emerged that shortly after the murder, Beale went out with friends for a drink and to play cards, another fact that makes his story of blind panic and anger seem a little dubious.

John Beale was hanged in Taunton on 12 January 1858. It is said that 10,000 people were present to witness the execution.

The Cinema Murder

ON 29 MAY 1946, WHILE THE FILM IN THE NEARBY AUDITORIUM WAS IN FULL FLOW, THE MANAGER OF A BRISTOL CINEMA WAS SHOT DEAD IN HIS OFFICE. THE KILLER HAS NEVER BEEN BROUGHT TO JUSTICE IN WHAT REMAINS BRISTOL'S OLDEST COLD CASE.

When in April 1946 Robert Parrington Jackson took over as manager of the Odeon in Bristol it was considered sufficiently newsworthy to appear on the front page of the *Western Daily Press*. At the end of the following month when the new manager was shot dead it was the national newspapers carrying the story.

In his twenties Parrington Jackson had found work as an actor in Hollywood. One of the parts he is said to have played was as one of the Merry Men in the Errol Flynn film *The Adventures of Robin Hood,* filmed over a period of four months from September 1937. Although the claim is probably true, it is a film with a great many heavily disguised extras and he is impossible to pick out. With the advent of war any burgeoning film career was put on hold.

With the outbreak of war Robert Parrington Jackson enlisted in The Royal Navy

© Bill Walden

With his war service over, Parrington Jackson sought work as a cinema manager. His first posting had been at the Newport Odeon, where he had been a popular figure, albeit that he was said to have something of an eye for the ladies. He then embarked on his brief stint as the manager of the Bristol Odeon.

On the evening of the murder, the audience were watching *The Light That Failed* and were oblivious to the crime. The film was based on a Rudyard Kipling story set in nineteenth-century Africa. A persistent story circulating is that the gunshot that killed Parrington Jackson coincided with a gunshot in the soundtrack of the film. If so it was exemplary timing as the film contains just one brief scene in which a number of shots are fired.

The Odeon in Broadmead, Bristol where the killing took place

Although back in 1946 the Odeon was a single auditorium (the current clothes shop on the site would have been the foyer of the cinema) it is comparatively easy to get an idea of the layout of the building. The window for the office where the shooting occurred was just above the canopy, to the right of the main entrance. It was in this office that Parrington Jackson put away the takings in the office safe. Detectives discovered that two shots had been fired; one missed but the other caused a fatal head wound. Parrington Jackson died at the Bristol Royal Infirmary, never regaining consciousness.

Superintendent Fred Carter of Bristol Constabulary took charge of the case, and one of the first obstacles he faced was finding a compelling motive. The keys to the safe remained in the victim's pocket and the money from the safe had not been taken.

Parrington Jackson's funeral was held a week later. A wreath was sent from J. Arthur Rank himself and people were clearly very much in shock. The new manager had just been starting to make his mark and had arranged for a special preview of the film *The Captive Heart*, which the Lord Mayor had been due to attend. This was now cancelled.

A series of suspects were taken in for questioning but no one was ever charged. Of particular interest in the aftermath of the crime was a man who was seen sitting on a settee in the Balcony Lounge at the top of the stairs from the foyer, more or less directly outside the office where the shooting occurred. This suspect came to be known as 'the long-faced man', described as having blue eyes and bad teeth and wearing a tatty suit. He was enjoying a cup of tea and sardines on toast in the period leading up to the murder.

On Saturday 1 June a reconstruction was staged with a police detective taking on the role of the assailant and trying out a possible exit strategy which involved leaving the manager's office by crawling along rafters inside the void of the cinema balcony. If this route was used by the long-faced man, rather than mingling in with the public, then he was obviously a great deal fitter than his sallow complexion had led the witnesses to believe.

Rumours at the time put the killing down to Mr Parrington Jackson being murdered by a jealous man who thought the manager had been flirting with his girlfriend. Others gossiped that it could have been the boyfriend of an usherette who had become pregnant by him. It may have loosely fitted Parrington Jackson's character but it did not tie in with the facts of the case. Surely the murder was more likely to be related to the cinema rather than to the victim. There would be plenty of other opportunities to take some sort of revenge without getting into the extraordinarily risky position of having to escape from a cinema having fired a gun.

The police always maintained that it had been a robbery that had gone wrong. As if to bear this out, in 1989 a small-time Welsh criminal apparently confessed to the killing on his deathbed. Four years later the matter was brought to the attention of the police by the son of the dead man. His story was that Parrington Jackson had returned to the office unexpectedly and in a moment of panic from the intruders he was shot dead. But something about the story did not ring true and, despite this alleged confession, officially the case remains unsolved.

Dreadful Murder at Weston-super-Mare

IN 1841 JOEL AND MARY FISHER MOVED TO THE DEVONSHIRE INN, LOCATED IN WESTON-SUPER-MARE HIGH STREET. JOEL HAD SERVED IN THE ARMY BUT DESPITE HIS MANY YEARS AWAY HE KNEW SOMERSET WELL. HE HAD BEEN BORN JUST TO THE NORTH IN WICK ST LAWRENCE AND IN A SENSE HE WAS COMING HOME. IT WAS AT THE DEVONSHIRE INN, THREE YEARS LATER, THAT MARY WAS MURDERED.

Joel Fisher's army career had been with the 7th Hussars, a cavalry regiment which during his time with them fought in the Peninsular War and at the Battle of Waterloo, where over half of the regiment were casualties. Fisher remained in the army for a further twenty years after the defeat of Napoleon, at which point the regiment was largely based in Ireland and Scotland. Eventually Joel left in order to take employment as a servant to one of his own ex-officers.

In a short space of time he had left the army, married a fellow servant and had two young children before becoming a widower after the sad death of his wife. It was then that he met Mary Hyatt. Mary had been married twice before and she too had two young children. Her second husband was a labourer called Thomas Hyatt, and she had been widowed at about the same time as Fisher lost his wife. Her first husband is more of a mystery, as he had a reputation for being something of a criminal and was prone to disappearing off the scene for long periods of time.

Fisher married Mary in September 1838 and from the outset there were monumental rows between the two of them. Despite this, and also Mary's brief sojourn back with her re-appearing first husband, they stayed together for the next six years.

On 3 June 1844, while Fisher was briefly away from the pub, Mary managed to have a huge argument with one of the lodgers, Peter Baker, who by the time that Joel returned had left and said that he had no intention of returning. Even though Baker was gone, Mary was still in the mood for arguing and the bickering continued throughout the day with Joel eventually becoming so incandescent with anger that Mary had to take refuge in the bedroom. Even then the argument raged on through the locked door.

The next morning at five o'clock Ann Evans, who was a live-in servant at the pub and had only been employed there for a fortnight, awoke to find Joel in the bedroom which she was now sharing with Mary, holding an iron bar. He assured Ann that she would not be harmed, before starting to beat Mary with the weapon. He then left the room for a couple of minutes before returning to cut her throat with a carving knife. Joel now entered the room of William Upsall, who was a local carpenter and the remaining lodger at the pub, and announced, 'William, I've done it!' Fisher told Upsall to go and get a policeman. On the way to the police station he also collected the local doctor. While the doctor confirmed that Mary was dead the policeman took Fisher into custody.

Fisher's trial took place on 12 August 1844. Despite the intervening weeks Fisher was showing no signs of contrition. The main defence was really based around the fact that Mary was so incredibly argumentative. Clearly, by itself, this was not going to earn Fisher any respite from the full force of the law, but there was the hope that the charge could be reduced to manslaughter. The defence argued that the attack was carried out in a totally brazen way, in front of witnesses. Surely this was evidence of a temporary insanity. However, Fisher was found guilty of murder.

While in gaol awaiting execution, the condemned man was allowed to see and say farewell to his family. To his eldest son he gave his Waterloo medal, telling him that he wished he had died at Waterloo and thus spared him this disgrace. Joel Fisher was hanged on 4 September

1844, outside the walls of Wilton Gaol in Taunton, at eleven o'clock in the morning. He faced his death with great bravery, in a manner befitting a Waterloo veteran, calmly climbing to the scaffold without a struggle.

The site on Weston-super-Mare High Street where once The Devonshire Inn stood Google Streetview

The Murder of Miss Jefferies

EARLY IN THE MORNING OF 3 MARCH 1849, SCREAMING COULD BE HEARD COMING FROM 6 TRENCHARD STREET IN BRISTOL, THE HOME OF ELIZABETH JEFFERIES. A COUPLE OF HOURS LATER THE NEIGHBOURS RECEIVED A VISIT FROM MISS JEFFERIES' SERVANT, SARAH THOMAS. SHE APOLOGISED FOR THE NOISE AND ASSURED THEM THAT THERE WAS NO NEED TO WORRY. THEY ACCEPTED THE EXPLANATION AND AS A RESULT IT WAS TO BE FOUR DAYS BEFORE MISS JEFFERIES' BODY WAS FOUND.

The early-morning visit to the neighbours had been the first time that they had met Sarah, who was the latest in a long line of Miss Jefferies' servants. Her predecessors had tended to swiftly move on as she was considered something of a difficult employer.

When a friend of Miss Jefferies came to visit her, the house in Trenchard Street appeared to be empty and was locked up. The last activity that any of the neighbours were able to report was of someone answering Sarah's description, together with a man, removing property from the house. There can be little doubt that this was indeed Sarah, whose next port of call was a nearby confectioner's shop where the owner was persuaded to look after a bundle of belongings which she said she would be along to collect later.

Sarah was next seen at her parents' house in Horfield. She arrived with rather more luggage than she normally had. She was soon back in central Bristol to collect the bundle from the shop, and then this too was taken by cab to Horfield. Sarah had a bit of a track record of petty pilfering but, even so, this amount of apparently stolen property was a completely new departure.

Back at Trenchard Street the body was discovered. Elizabeth Jefferies had been beaten to death with a heavy doorstop. The police now went in search of Sarah. One of the first places they looked was Sarah's mother's house, where a fairly cursory search quickly revealed that Sarah was hiding in the coal hole. Equally easy to recover was the huge haul of jewellery and money that had originated from Miss Jefferies' house.

Sarah's explanation was that the attack and robbery must have been carried out by one of Miss Jefferies' relations. This seemed unlikely as she was estranged from her family, who would seldom visit. When this story didn't seem to go down well, she came out with a further version which involved a disgruntled servant, called Maria, returning to the house to exact revenge.

The spoils of the robbery that were found in Sarah's possession were explained away as being a present from Maria. A search was now conducted to find anyone called Maria who had a connection to Trenchard Street. Previous servants were quick to support Sarah's assertion as to the filthy temper of Miss Jefferies, but they all had alibis and none of them were called Maria.

At Sarah's trial she seemed to quite enjoy all the attention that was coming her way, and apparently didn't realise just how much trouble she was actually in. A glimmer of hope came from just one witness who now came forward. This was a young girl of eleven years of age (some reports say as young as nine) called Ann Sullivan. Ann knew Sarah and was able to report that since Christmas she knew that Sarah had been seeing a soldier and that he was also involved in the robbery. On the day of Miss Jefferies' murder she had been in a local pub called the Flitch of Bacon, which from Trenchard Street would be the other side of where the Colston Hall now stands, in Host Street. There this new witness had seen a man called Matthew Lyon and two riflemen (one of whom was Sarah's new friend), and they were clearly plotting a murder. She also claimed to have witnessed a portion of the attack and stated that Lyon was quite clearly the leader.

There might have been some defence of Sarah to be made by saying that she had been part of a gang, with her job simply being to gain them admittance to Miss Jefferies' house. After all, there was the mysterious accomplice who was seen to help her carry away the heavier items. By this time a set of keys to number 6 had been found in a groove in the shutters of the pub where the plan was supposed to have been hatched. They could have been left by Sarah on her return trip to Trenchard Street, or there could have been a different explanation involving an accomplice.

Unfortunately Ann may have pushed her luck with some of the more fantastic details and inaccuracies of her testimony. Soon she was claiming that she had followed the gang into the house, guided by a blind uncle, and saw one of the soldiers cut off the old woman's head with his sword. This was clearly complete nonsense and her testimony was stopped with her still in full flow. If there is any grain of truth in her story then it was lost under layers of fanciful imaginings.

It appeared that the heavy doorstop that was used to bludgeon the victim had been taken upstairs in preparation for the attack and so any hope of saving Sarah from the gallows, by demonstrating a lack of premeditation, was lost. Sarah was found guilty of murder.

Prior to being hanged on Friday 20 April 1849 Sarah did confess to the murder and said that she acted alone. The man who had been observed assisting her was supposedly just a stranger whom she had paid for helping to move the stolen goods. She still had no explanation for the set of keys to number 6 which she said she had simply thrown away in the street.

The surviving gatehouse of the New Gaol in Bristol where Sarah Thomas was executed

A selection of other books for you to enjoy from Bradwell Books from around the South West

Somerset

Bradwell's Pocket Walking Guide Somerset
ISBN13: 9781910551912

Bradwell's Somerset Tales & Trivia
ISBN13: 9781910551325

Legends & Folklore Somerset
ISBN13: 9781910551516

Somerset & Bristol Murder Stories
ISBN13: 9781912060603

Somerset Dialect: A Selection of Words and
Anecdotes from Around Somerset
ISBN13: 9781902674896

Somerset Ghost Stories
ISBN13: 9781909914490

Somerset Wit & Humour
ISBN13: 9781909914681

Walks for All Ages Somerset: 19 Short Walks for
All the Family
ISBN13: 9781909914803

Bristol Dialect: A Selection of Words and
Anecdotes from Around Bristol
ISBN13: 9781909914230

Cornwall

Bradwell's Images of Cornwall
ISBN13: 9781909914773

Bradwell's Images of Cornwall: German
Translation
ISBN13: 9781909914841

Bradwells Book of Cornwall
ISBN13: 9781912060580

Colour Cornwall
ISBN13: 9781912060511

Cornish Dialect: A Selection of Words and
Anecdotes from Around Cornwall
ISBN13: 9781902674353

Cornish Ghost Stories: Shiver Your Way Around
Cornwall
ISBN13: 9781902674476

Legends & Folklore Cornwall
ISBN13: 9781912060696

South West Murder Stories: A selection of grizzly
stories from around Devon & Cornwall
ISBN13: 9781912060979

Walks for All Ages in Cornwall: 20 Short Walks
for All the Family
ISBN13: 9781902674780

Cornish Dialect: A Selection of Words and
Anecdotes from Around Cornwall
ISBN13: 9781902674353

Cornish Ghost Stories: Shiver Your Way Around
Cornwall
ISBN13: 9781902674476

Cornish Wit & Humour
ISBN13: 9781910551035

Colour Dorset
ISBN13: 9781912060764

Devon

Bradwell's Images of Devon
ISBN13: 9781910551479

Devon Dialect: A Selection of Words and
Anecdotes from Around Devon
ISBN13: 9781909914001

Devon Wit & Humour
ISBN13: 9781910551042

South West Murder Stories: A selection of grizzly
stories from around Devon & Cornwall
ISBN13: 9781912060979

Walks for All Ages in Devon: 20 Short Walks for
All the Family
ISBN13: 9781909914919

Dorset

Dorset Dialect
ISBN13: 9781910551011

Dorset Ghost Stories
ISBN13: 9781909914469

Dorset Wit & Humour
ISBN13: 9781909914650

Legends & Folklore Dorset
ISBN13: 9781910551493

Tales & Trivia Dorset
ISBN13: 9781910551301

Walks for All Ages Dorset: 20 Short Walks for
All the Family
ISBN13: 9781909914339

Wessex Murder Stories: A selection of grizzly stories
from around Dorset, Hampshire & Wiltshire
ISBN13: 9781912060610

Wiltshire

Bradwell's Wiltshire Tales & Trivia
ISBN13: 9781910551332

Legends & Folklore Wiltshire
ISBN13: 9781910551004

Walks for All Ages Wiltshire: 20 Short Walks for
All the Family
ISBN13: 9781909914704

Wessex Murder Stories: A selection of grizzly stories
from around Dorset, Hampshire & Wiltshire
ISBN13: 9781912060610

Wiltshire Dialect
ISBN13: 9781909914605

Wiltshire Ghost Stories
ISBN13: 9781909914964

Wiltshire Wit & Humour
ISBN13: 9781909914568

Search on line at bradwellbooks.co.uk
Follow us on Twitter - @bradwellbooks
Like us on Facebook – Bradwell Books